A Touch of Greatness

By C. W. ANDERSON

NEW YORK 1945

THE MACMILLAN COMPANY

Foreword

Turf history is emblazoned with the great names that have adorned it—Man o' War, Colin, Sysonby, Exterminator, Count Fleet —but a little applause should be reserved for those not so richly endowed by nature who yet performed splendidly. Out of lesser cloth they fashioned their banners, substituting honesty for speed or courage for stamina. These are not great horses, perhaps, but of what they had they gave generously, often overcoming natural handicaps to give thrilling performances. They had color, appeal and, at least, a touch of greatness.

Contents

Display—BAD BOY MAKES GOOD

One August day in 1944, in a stall padded halfway up the sides, death quenched a fiery spirit that life had never been able to tame. Racing papers carried the news under the heading, "The Iron Horse Dies."

Probably more than one former assistant starter felt the rheumatic twinge of an old injury in an arm or shoulder as he read the news, and with it a feeling of regret at the passing of a worthy adversary, for this was the Bad Boy of all Bad Boys, the worst post horse of our time. Here was an irreconcilable rebel who never learned the meaning of compromise.

From the day his legs lost the shaky uncertainty of youth until the day he died, this tough bay horse never backed a step for man or beast. He wasted enough energy fighting the ground crew at the barrier to have completely worn out and eliminated a lesser horse from any racing chance.

Despite this, he stood at the top of money winners in his day. The average horse of Stakes caliber will run from twenty to forty races by the time he is retired. Display ran 103 races! He earned his name of Iron Horse the hard way.

The temperaments and dispositions of horses, and their various manifestations, is one of the most interesting of studies. There is almost as great a range of variance as in people and if you merely group them under the headings of "well mannered" horses and "bad actors," you are scarcely more definite than if you divided the human race into good people and bad people.

Some horses are so amiable that they will obey blindly, with an almost nervous eagerness to anticipate your wishes. Some are intelligent enough to obey only if what they are asked is reasonable or in line with previous experience and training. Others obey grudgingly and, if they sense any uncertainty, will immediately take advantage of it. Bluffers at heart, they will immediately back down in the face of discipline.

There are a few horses that are naturally mean and treacherous and thoroughly undependable, regardless of training. Beyond are those so high spirited as to be difficult, that must be handled with skill and patience rather than force.

This kind the English call "high couraged." It is not a bad designation, for great competitive spirit and courage nearly always accompany such dispositions. Among these are found a few that have such a rebellious, independent nature that compulsion is like a red flag. They will fight to the last rather than submit to force. This, raised to the nth degree, was Display—rugged, brilliant, moody, temperamental son of the immortal Fair Play.

Display was never mean or tricky. He just planted his four feet solidly and, with head high, dared you to force him to do anything he did not want to do. When Man o' War's exercise boy said of Big Red, "You got to ask him, not push him," he might have been speaking of Display, except that in his case it would have been a good idea to say "Please" also.

Thoroughbred temperament has always been a subject of discussion and argument among horsemen. At such times the Fair Plays are usually in the lead, for their fiery impetuosity is widely known. Nearly all of them, even to the third and fourth generation, have a trace of this fire.

Fair Play was an amazingly prepotent sire and his characteristics are often strongly stamped on a colt with any trace of his blood. This temperament is most often seen at the barrier, as would be natural, for a high-spirited horse is most impatient to be at the business of racing and resents all the delay and restraints. Running at top speed is in his blood. Standing quietly at the barrier is not.

The methods used to compel this obedience usually make a high-spirited horse's behavior worse. There is not much time to be patient and, at best, starting crews are not overly gentle in handling rebellious horses. At the first sign of recalcitrance the punishing twitch is put on the nose, which is a horse's most sensitive spot. The great Equipoise, who was such a model of behavior at all other times, grew to hate the starters and often fought like a demon when handled by them.

The electric starting gate has helped in eliminating both bad behavior by the horses and manhandling of fractious animals. Many horses that would never stand quietly in the open, at the old type of barrier, are well behaved in the stall gate. Yet it is doubtful if it would have had any effect on Display. Under any conditions the start calls for complete obedience with force in instant attendance. No matter how presented this would always have been poison to Display. The handling he received at the barrier probably did no more than accentuate what was already there, for he always had the look of a horse with a will of his own.

Display showed early promise, winning his second start as a two-year-old. He was then shipped to Canada, where he was champion in his division, winning six of seven starts. Going to Maryland in the fall he was third in the Pimlico Futurity. Improving over that effort, he was beaten only a head by the speedy Man o' War colt, Mars, in the Walden Handicap. Since the Fair Plays are traditionally slow in developing, this was a very creditable two-year-old campaign, and Display went into winter quarters as a nice prospect for the three-year-old classics.

He was pointed for the Preakness the next spring, as that stake was then run a week before the Derby. In preparation for this big race he was entered in an overnight event at a mile and a sixteenth. That was the time to start to separate the sprinters from the stayers and many brilliant two-year-old winners began to fade out of the picture as the distances were stretched out. Display, however, won his race and finished so stoutly that there seemed little doubt that he would be benefited by the longer routes of the three-year-old stakes.

Post time on Preakness day found a large field starting in the rich stake and a number of the colts were so highly considered by the public that Display's chances were entirely overlooked. He was held at 18 to 1 in the betting. Bradley, who has made a sort of habit of winning Derbys and Preakness Stakes, had Baggenbaggage entered, and he shared favoritism with the well tried colts, Blondin and Canter.

The race proved one of the most exciting in the long list of thrilling contests on the Preakness roster. The two favorites, Baggenbaggage and Canter, were off with the first flight. At the three-quarters pole they were right in the pace, while Display and Blondin, who were off poorly, were well back in the second division. As the field turned into the stretch, some of the front runners began to weaken and Display, coming strongly, slipped through an opening on the rail and was at the leaders in a few strides.

Blondin, who had been running head and head with Display all the way, went around tiring horses and was again at Display's throatlatch, where he stuck all through the stretch, unable to gain another inch.

The two horses went under the wire in exactly the same position, with Display the winner by a head.

That long-stretch drive stamped the bay colt as a courageous horse, for the faint-hearted ones rarely can withstand so prolonged a challenge. Often in his later career Display failed to run his race; often he sulked or refused to extend himself, but it can never be said that he quit. His temper has been criticized but his courage was never questioned.

The Derby the following week was one of those reversals that simply cannot be explained. Again Blondin and Display ran as a team, head and head, all the way. This time they finished ninth and tenth instead of first and second. Display was already

becoming a problem child at the barrier and he may well have helped his own defeat by his behavior. Why Blondin should have finished so far back of the same field he had outclassed a week earlier is one of those mysteries that makes every horse race a contest until the wire is reached.

Display's only other stake victory was in the Latonia Championship Stakes, where he beat Bradley's good horse, Boot to Boot. However, he showed well in other big events, being second in the American Derby, the Cincinnati Derby and the Saratoga Cup and he placed in a number of other stakes. While training for the Bryan Memorial he injured himself and was retired for the season. For a horse that always spent his energies so prodigally before the racing began, it was a good campaign.

The following year, as a four-year-old, he was a much better horse. He had to be, for his post behavior was now wilder and more acrobatic than ever. Had he been of a different temperament it is hard to estimate just how great he might have been, for only a horse with at least a touch of real greatness could have spent fifteen minutes in rearing and plunging under top weight, dragging a couple of 200-pound assistant starters all over the track, and still have enough left to come on and win in the stretch.

Perhaps his greatest accomplishment of the year was winning the Washington Handicap, for behind him that day were the great Crusader, as well as Mars, Black Maria, Jock and Gaffsman, each a star in his own right. Besides this he won the Toronto Cup, the Champlain Handicap, the Baltimore Handicap, and the Pimlico Cup. That he was a true stayer was very obvious by now, and his victory in the Pimlico Cup at two miles and a quarter gave still further proof of this fact. He was one horse that was always benefited by the added furlongs. A mile and a quarter, which is beyond the limit of so many of our present-day horses, was almost too short for him to be at his best.

At five Display reached his peak—on those few occasions when he kept his mind on racing and got off anywhere near his field. It was that year he won the Hawthorne

Gold Cup, setting a new track record and beating Crusader and Mike Hall at even weights. While it should be stated that Crusader was not at his best, for he never again was the same horse after being severely kicked at the post, he was still no mean adversary, and Mike Hall was a very rugged sort of campaigner with many good races to his credit.

Display also won the Toronto Cup Handicap for the second year, but in between these winning performances he tossed away race after race by the violence of his battles at the barrier. There was now open warfare between the big bay and the starters and while Display never lost a battle to them, it was at the cost of many a race, for it was often beyond the powers of even an Iron Horse to win two victories the same afternoon.

In his six-year-old campaign he won three races before a foot injury compelled his retirement. He showed versatility in his last race when he won the Baltimore Handicap at a mile and seventy yards—mere sprinting distance for him. While training for the rich Agua Caliente Handicap, in which his

chances seemed excellent, he went wrong. It was announced he would continue racing the following year, but that statement was made without consulting Display.

He was used as a stallion for the rest of that breeding season and from the small handful of foals in his first, and rather accidental, season at stud came that big handsome handicap star, Discovery. The Iron Horse outbred himself in almost his first mating and never again did he approach it. But a Discovery does not come along every day, or even every decade.

In the spring Display was again sent into training quarters, but he had made up his mind he was through with racing, and, as he thoroughly demonstrated, it was foolish of mere man to try to change his plans. No one could get him to extend himself. It was as if he had decided he had done his stint and no one was going to make him do more. True, his name appeared in the entries and he was led onto the track on four occasions, but they might as well have left him in the stable. The tough bay horse with legs like iron had a will that was cast in the same mold.

He was retired permanently to the stud with total earnings on the track of $256,326, all of which, with the exception of the Preakness purse, was earned in the hardest way— in the handicaps.

Many a horse that wins a $50,000 handicap today would not have been in the money in races Display won, which earned him but one tenth that sum. There were giants in those days, and plenty of them.

As a sire, Display was successful, although he produced but one horse that could be called first class. He got his share of winners and if most of his sons and daughters had enough of his temperament for it to be considered a drawback, they made up for this by their rugged constitutions and durability. It is not unusual to find the Displays campaigning season after season against younger horses, for almost all their contemporaries have fallen by the wayside.

Display's son, Supply House, was a good horse and won many rich stakes, while Volitant, who looked so promising as a two-year-old, was too undependable later to live up to his early promise. He inherited a little too much of his sire's temperament and he is still the bane of the handicapper's existence. Only God and Volitant know if he will decide to run his race when he goes to the post and it is often pretty clear that Volitant himself isn't entirely certain.

Among Display's other stakes winners are Sabin, Fast Stride, Driver, Winter Sport, Parade Girl, Sobriety and Mistress Plato. Among the lesser ones, that could best be described as "useful" horses, there are many that have won twenty-five to thirty-five races, which would indicate campaigns of more than a hundred races. Horses of such durability and soundness are a boon to the small trainer, who lives from purse to purse. Undoubtedly these breadwinners are forgiven whims and temperament without too much ado.

But if Display had done no more than sire the blaze-faced, golden-coated Discovery, he would always be entitled to a place among fine sires. Here was such a performer as Display himself might have been if only he had had his son's gentler temper. Big, of almost faultless conformation, one of the greatest weight carriers of our generation, Discovery had both tremendous speed and great stamina. He carried 139 pounds and won with it. Had he been racing today, when it is almost an unwritten law that the top horse in a handicap carries no more than 130 pounds, he might have been the greatest money winner of them all. Time and again he gave away fifteen or twenty lengths, in weight, and was beaten by the narrowest of margins.

He had one weakness that other riders often took advantage of to defeat him—he sometimes sulked if he was repeatedly bumped and crowded in a race. There was no "quit" in Display's handsome son but he knew the rules and if he was given more than his share of unfair handicaps he sometimes decided to call it a day. An intelligent horse realizes that he can't be knocked off stride repeatedly under staggering weights and still have a chance to win, and Discovery was nothing if not intelligent. Whenever the handicapper was lenient with him—anything under 135 pounds almost assured Discovery of victory—he always hung up sensational time. His mile and three sixteenths in 1:55 is still something for our light-weighted racers to shoot at.

On the stud farm Display was not the terror he was at the track, but he was still no angel child. One look at the big bay and the veriest tyro would know that here was not a horse that would come nuzzling you for sugar. If things did not suit him in his stall he beat such a violent tattoo on the planks that the stall was padded halfway up both sides to protect him and to deaden the sound of those protests of the eternal rebel.

Most stallions are turned out in a paddock for half the day when the weather permits, but this could not be done with Display. After an hour he would become bored, or perhaps be attacked by claustrophobia, and begin to kick the planks out of the fences. The song that goes "I can't look at hobbles and I can't stand fences," might have been written for Display.

But he was never a dangerous horse for a groom to handle, such as the savages and maneaters that we read of in the old days. It would be interesting if we could trace back, step by step, changes that take place in a tough horse's disposition and find out how much is hereditary, or ingrained, and how much was created by man. The great differences of opinion can be seen in respect to Leamington, sire of the great Lexington, who was reputed to be a completely vicious horse and was generally known as a "maneater." Yet John McClosky, his stud groom, said of him: "He was a horse of great high spirits and liked to show his heels if things did not suit him, but he was not vicious. I have often lain down in his box, when he would come up and rub his nose all over my face and lick it with his tongue." And then he added mildly, "Of course he had his likes and dislikes."

A similar case was that of the English horse, Cruiser, which had a reputation as the most dangerous horse in all England, 100 years ago. He nearly killed several men and became so violent that no attempt was made to get him out of his stall. A small opening was made in the door through which to feed him and he wore a heavy iron muzzle at all times.

At this time a young American, named John Rarey, was performing amazing feats in taming savage horses, and doing it with little use of force and no resort to punishment. In response to a challenge published in the press, he agreed to try his hand with Cruiser. Using hobbles he finally managed to get the raging animal down and helpless, then he spent an hour handling and caressing him, paying particular attention to the head and muzzle.

Later that afternoon Rarey rode the horse, which had not been outside of his stall in three years, to London. Within a few weeks he was exhibiting Cruiser to huge crowds at the Crystal Palace, with Queen Victoria in the enthusiastic audience. Few could believe, at first, that the horse that followed Rarey like a dog and obeyed at a word, was the vicious killer whose dangerous reputation was almost a legend. The strangest part of the story is that Rarey maintained to the day of his death that Cruiser, whom he acquired, was the most intelligent and affectionate horse he had ever known.

That these were not empty words, spoken for effect, was proved by the fact that Rarey's will made provision for Cruiser. The estate was so apportioned that a fund assured the horse the kindest care as long as he lived. Obviously, sometime in this horse's career he had been subjected to treatment that changed a high-spirited, intelligent animal into a dangerous beast. With such a horse, one brutal, violent encounter would be the spark to light a fire that could rise to a consuming fury.

Always when Display is mentioned, there is voiced the regret that his temper was such a handicap to his performance. This was undoubtedly true, but there may have been some compensation. Among the Fair Plays, their fire was so closely allied to the stamina and courage for which they were noted, that it is hard to be sure a milder temperament would be accompanied by that same blazing competitive spirit which has so strongly characterized that hardy tribe. Display had this spirit to an intense degree and in many a hard stretch duel it stood him in good stead. Perhaps the ledger was more nearly balanced than we know.

Even death came as it should for the horse that was born with a chip on his shoulder. Such an individual should not waste away from old age or succumb to the common ailments of colic or digestive troubles. The tough, independent son of Fair Play died of a heart attack.

Marriage—POOR START, GOOD FINISH

There is a great difference of opinion regarding marriage as an institution. There is very little in regard to the merits of Marriage, the horse.

Many a marriage starts off with a great fanfare and ends in a complete fiasco. The handsome blaze-faced chestnut gelding named Marriage started off poorly and ended in a blaze of glory. Starting in the cheapest of claiming races, he won his way into the rank of handicap stars.

It has been said that a difference of opinion makes horse racing. A group of horses equally matched is also a necessary ingredient. This is not so easy of attainment as might be assumed. After one horse has clearly demonstrated that he is the best of a group, the difference of opinion ceases to exist. So would racing within that group if nothing were done to equalize matters.

It is here the handicapper steps in. He so arranges weights that the best horse carries the most, with the others so weighted that they will have an equal chance. Theoretically, a well handicapped field of horses should reach the finish line in a dead heat. Practically, the handicapper has done an excellent job if not more than a dozen lengths separate the first and last horse, for horses are individuals and not machines. A good horse may summon enough reserve strength to neutralize weight that should have brought him back to those of lesser quality—a mediocre one may still be mediocre despite the weight conceded to him.

It is as a star in this handicap group that Marriage now finds himself. His quality and performances are such that he usually has to concede weight to his rivals. Only a few years ago he would not have qualified for the lowest grading of the handicap division.

The claiming races were designed to fit conditions for horses below the class of the handicaps and in them the owner handicaps his own horse to a great degree. Each horse entered in a claiming race has a price placed on him and he can be "claimed," or taken by another owner, at that price. Under this arrangement an owner or trainer is prevented from entering a horse that outclasses his field, for in doing so he would risk losing his horse at a price far below his true value. The cheapest of these claiming races at the important tracks is for $1000 platers and it was in this lowly company that Marriage began his career.

He is a well bred horse, being by the imported English stallion, Strolling Player, who traced back in top line to the great Ormonde. His dam was War Wedding, who was by Man o' War. This blood certainly could not be faulted, but for a long time it looked as if Misalliance might have been a better name for him than Marriage. Sold at auction as a two-year-old, in 1938, he brought $5300, a price his owner soon regretted, for in ten starts the chestnut colt won but one small purse. This is not the kind of racer that "wins himself out," or even pays his feed bill.

Marriage did not improve noticeably the following year. He was not raced at four and when he came back to the races at five he was a gelding. His first appearance was in a cheap claimer, with a price of $1000 on him. Evidently his owner had become discouraged with him, but he was too pessimistic, for the horse won and was claimed at his entered price.

The chestnut gelding's next start was in slightly better company. His price tag now was $1400 and he won easily. When he was claimed by that astute trainer, Hirsch Jacobs, it was evident to everyone that the horse was improving, for that canny horseman rarely makes a mistake in judging a horse's capabilities.

Under Jacobs' tutelage Marriage did very well, winning a string of six consecutive victories. After this his luck seemed to turn, for four defeats followed before the horse again entered the winner's circle. However, four more defeats in rapid succession might have made Jacobs feel that he could safely risk the gelding in a claimer, for he entered him with a price of $5000 on his head. That clever trainer guessed wrong for once, for Marriage was promptly claimed by R. A. Coward, who still owns him. To this day, Jacobs bitterly regrets having risked the horse in a claimer, for he knew that Marriage had not yet reached his best form.

Mr. Coward was also a smart horseman and he never repeated Jacobs' mistake of putting Marriage in a claimer. In a way it seems like a bit of poetic justice that a horse with as much "color" as this should be owned by a man who is also far from being a drab, conventional figure.

Coward was a prosperous furniture dealer in Dallas, Texas, when he began dabbling in racing in a small way. Soon his interest became so great that he gave up his furniture business and adopted the life of a "gyp" trainer, campaigning around the smaller tracks. "Gyp" is short for "gypsy" around the tracks—not a synonym for an overly shrewd manipulator, although the term can occasionally serve double duty without any great inaccuracy.

When Coward first invaded the New England tracks with his small string of horses he encountered a pretty hard-bitten crew of ex-harness racing men who knew every trick in the game, or thought they did. They looked upon the portly, bland-appearing Coward as a babe in the woods and he did nothing to disillusion them. A little later he entered a horse in a claiming race at a price that seemed much too low. A number of trainers prepared to put in a claim for the horse. The word got around to Coward and on the morning of the race he appeared with a doleful face at the stable of one of the trainers who had let it be known that he intended to enter a claim for Coward's horse, and asked to borrow a tub to ice the horse's bad leg.

Repeating the performance at the other stables, where halters were ready for his horse, Coward brought back the tubs and piled them in a corner of his stable. Since he had sworn each trainer to secrecy, the word got around very quickly that he was running a bad-legged horse. When the horse came home in front, just breezing, there was not a single claim for him in the box. Since then the notion is pretty prevalent that the stout Texan knows his way around a race track.

Not long after Marriage had passed into Coward's hands he turned up in California. Now he was stepping up into select company, for he was entered in the Marchbank Handicap, with a purse of $15,000. From now on Marriage's rise to success takes on a distinct Horatio Alger twist and it is highly appropriate that the beginning of the meteoric rise of the cheap plater should take place in Hollywood's backyard, where the impossible is only the trite and conventional occurrence.

Marriage not only won the race but the time he hung out, of 1:49 for a mile and an eighth, is very close to the record on any track. As a result, the chestnut gelding that won less than $1000 in his first season made a record of twelve victories in nineteen starts, with total earnings for the year of $30,000. If the tale ended here it would not be a bad success story, but this is only the first chapter, for occasionally fact is more florid than fiction.

An even more ambitious program had been planned for the former plater for the winter—nothing less than a try at our richest race, the $100,000 Santa Anita Handicap. War conditions caused the cancellation of Pacific Coast race meetings and Marriage was shipped to Oaklawn Park, Arkansas. He was slow to round into form and did little in his first starts, which were obviously intended to prepare him for more important stakes later on. Coming back east he was beaten in his first start at Jamaica. The next time out he showed the beginning of a return to form, winning a $3500 handicap.

The following week Marriage went to the post in his first important stakes event of the year. He was one of eleven that went postward in the Grey Lag Handicap with a purse value of more than $15,000. In the field were many starters, including Market Wise, Tola Rose, The Rhymer, and Pictor—a class of competition he had not heretofore encountered. Aided by a light impost and a muddy track, which he always favored, he led all the way, beating the top-weighted Market Wise by three lengths. He was getting sixteen pounds from Market Wise—enough to explain his victory over that stout campaigner—but for him to be in the hunt at all against such a field was a real accomplishment. It bespoke an undreamed-of improvement.

Two weeks later, at Detroit, he ran another fine race, beaten only a head in the Inaugural Handicap. The following week Marriage showed that his improvement was no fluke, for he beat the good horse, Best Seller, at even weights in time only two fifths of a second off the track record. But it was later, at Chicago, that he showed how far he had really come.

The Grasslands Handicap was something of an innovation, for it was run over a turf course laid out in the infield, a kind of surface always used abroad, although little known in the United States. Usually a horse accustomed to our dirt tracks must race on the turf several times before he is at home on it.

Marriage took to it like a veteran and went to the front at once. Shaking off all challenges he set a fast pace and galloped home three lengths in front. The time showed a new American turf record of 2:02 2/5, time rarely made at a mile and a quarter on our fastest dirt tracks.

It might seem that a $1000 horse could now rest on his laurels but greater things were to come. The chestnut gelding was to be entered for the $25,000 Washington Park Handicap. In the field were the finest handicap horses in America, including the sensational Alsab, who was at the top of his form. In preparation for this important stake, Marriage was sent out in a mile event as a "tightener" for the big race. Taking up top weight he ran the distance in the impressive time of 1:36 4/5; which is flying on anybody's track.

That this fine effort did not gain him enough support to rank him with the favorites in the betting was due to the quality of the field. Alsab, a great Chicago favorite, had just won the American Derby in slashing style, while Thumbs Up and With Regards were dangerous in any race.

With Regards, whose speed was always exceptional, set a blazing pace from the start, leading to the mile pole in the sensational time of 1:36. Here his effort began to tell on him and when Thumbs Up drew up beside him he could not withstand the challenge and the high-headed bay went past him. At this point Marriage began his move and Alsab from farther back also began his drive. Thumbs Up fought courageously to hold the lead but the charge of the chestnut was too much and Marriage moved past, going into a lead by open daylight.

Alsab, under top weight, was coming fast but although he collared Thumbs Up in the last strides, he could not catch Marriage, going so smoothly in front.

As they went under the wire Marriage still had a length lead and he was running strongly. The time was only 2/5 of a second behind the track record. This was Marriage's finest performance to date, and it stamped him as a real handicap star, for it takes a good horse to come off of such a pace as a mile in 1:36 and have winning speed left in the final furlongs.

Marriage was never a rugged sort of horse and trained "light." When he went off form it took considerable time to bring him back fresh and fit, but when he was in good condition he was a horse of rare consistency. In his last five races—all of them handicaps against very strong fields—he won four and was beaten in the other only a head.

Few of the top-notchers can show such consistent performance, and the chestnut speedster was not yet through. Three weeks later he stepped out at Belmont Park. Taking up top weight in his field he ran one of the fastest mile and a furlong races ever recorded in this country. In doing this he was at the mile in 1:35 3/5—time that is recorded in the mile events only once in a blue moon. He finished out the mile and an eighth in the new

track record time of 1:48 1/5! When horses even shade 1:50 for that distance it usually makes the headlines.

Several subsequent races showed he needed a rest. No wonder, for he had been going since early winter and had been meeting the toughest sort of opposition. When it was apparent that he had lost his form he was taken out of training to be rested and freshened. His earnings for the year had doubled those of his previous season with more than $60,000 to his credit. In accomplishing this he had at one time or another beaten practically every top handicap star in training.

The next year's campaign was one of ups and downs. Although it contained one of Marriage's most brilliant victories and the richest purse he had ever won, there was also a larger proportion of defeats. He did not have a long winter's rest. His last race of 1942 was run on December 12 and on February 22 he was again facing the starter at the Fair Grounds in New Orleans. He appeared to be "short" in this his first race of the year, for he tired at the end instead of finishing with his usual dash and resolution.

Apparently it was thought that the old gelding was all washed up, for he was now seven, which is old for a race horse. When he paraded to the post for the New Orleans Handicap he was not only an outsider but a longshot at odds of 37 to 1. That the slim son of Strolling Player was not going to take this insult lying down was soon apparent, for when the field came into the stretch Marriage was seen coming with great speed. In the drive to the wire he won by open daylight. Behind him were such fine horses as Riverland, Mioland, Requested and Rounders and the time hung out equaled the track record.

There still was life in the old horse. If he had reached his peak and was on the way down, it was pretty clear that the descent was not going to be a toboggan slide.

In March, Marriage again met Mioland in the $10,000 American Handicap. He proved that his previous victory over the husky Pacific Coast star was no fluke, for he set all the pace and stood off the powerful challenge of Mioland all through the stretch to win by a nose. Since there was but a pound difference in their imposts, this was an especially fine performance. It takes more out of a horse to set the pace and then stand off challenges than to follow it and come from behind.

Rarely did Marriage lose a close decision even though it was a head-and-head drive all through the stretch. That is the mark of a really game horse. In this respect he resembles that other gamester, Market Wise, whose career is so similar to that of Marriage. Both started from the lowest rung, both gained the top the hard way and both were at their best when the going was tough.

After a very creditable second to the powerful Devil Diver in both the Carter and Metropolitan Handicaps, at distances too short to give Marriage his best opportunities, he returned to Chicago. On July 5 he was one of the field for the $50,000 Stars and Stripes Handicap and although he did not win, he was a good third, beaten only a length. This set the stage for his richest triumph, the renewal of the $50,000 Arlington Handicap. Carrying 120 pounds against a good field, he was close to the pace from the start. He took over at the mile pole and led all the way home to win by a length.

Here we can well leave Marriage—a lowly plater valued at but $1000 a few years before, winning a $50,000 handicap. His full career on the track is not yet over but at his age it is doubtful if he can add many more great triumphs to his score. He has earned the right to have his story end on a high note. His total earnings are more than $200,000.

Marriage is a very appealing animal with an unusually intelligent head and a fine shoulder. His color is such a light golden chestnut that it is easy to pick him out in a field, even if there are many chestnut horses included. Some horsemen have a strong aversion to a horse whose color is of a light shade, claiming that it is a mark of weakness. But most trainers would love to have a stableful of horses with the sort of weakness that Marriage had.

Market Wise—A TRUE FAIRY TALE

The story of Market Wise is the story of rags to riches with extra embellishments—the lily is gilded beyond recognition. If it were fiction it would require a very florid Hollywood writer to imagine such a tale. As a result, the story will be told with as much restraint as possible, in order to give it some semblance of reality.

Broker's Tip, who sired Market Wise, had never entered the winner's circle at either two or three, and his presence in the Kentucky Derby field of 1933 was a forlorn hope indeed. Possibly Colonel Bradley merely wanted to see his colors up in a race that had meant so much to him, for he had won three times with horses of his own breeding.

The race itself stands alone in turf history as the wildest, roughest, most unorthodox race ever run. All through the stretch Meade on Broker's Tip and Fischer on Head Play were fighting it out, slashing at each other with their whips, kicking, grabbing at the saddle cloths and letting the horses run as best they might. The horses crossed the line nose and nose, literally locked in a struggle.

By all rules of racing, both horses should have been disqualified but after a long delay the race was given to Broker's Tip and both riders were suspended for long periods.

Head Play proved himself the better horse, for he won the Preakness, the Suburban, and other stakes, while Broker's Tip never again won a race. When he broke down and had to be retired, Colonel Bradley did not want him for the stud and he was put up at auction.

He brought only $1400—the price of a very cheap plater. That such a horse would be used at stud at all is strange; that he would produce anything of any account seemed utterly impossible. Yet when bred to a mare named On Hand, he produced Market Wise, a horse that in his best form had few equals in his day.

Most of the quality that Market Wise possessed must have come from the dam, for she produced a number of good horses when bred to other sires. Possibly Broker's Tip merely transmitted the virtues of his own sire, Black Toney, a famous and successful stallion. At any rate there are few instances on record of a horse outbreeding himself by such a tremendous margin.

That Market Wise had more than a touch of greatness will be clear to those who have followed his career. In fact, it was only because he was never entirely sound that his record is not more impressive. He was light boned and his hoofs were not too durable, so that it was often necessary to send him to the races without the amount of work that a more rugged horse would have been given. To train a sound horse and always have him at his peak for his races is difficult enough, but to do it with an unsound one that must be nursed along, is far more exacting. If Market Wise's record of nineteen victories in fifty-three starts does not sound impressive alongside those of horses that were rarely beaten, it should be remembered that an unbeaten horse is usually a thoroughly sound one.

The first appearance of Market Wise under colors was not brilliant. In a race for maiden two-year-olds at Saratoga, twenty-one started and he finished twentieth. In his next start he finished last. In his third he was seventeenth. Dropped into a claiming race, out of which he could have been taken for $1500, he could do no better than sixth. If there was an uglier ugly duckling no one knew of it, so it is not surprising that he was for sale.

His breeding was undistinguished and gave little promise of more than his dreary performances indicated. When Louis Tufano wanted to buy a colt named Flank, Market Wise was tossed in to boot, so to speak. The price was $2000. Flank proved worthless but Market Wise earned $222,000.

His first start for his new owner was in a claimer against very common horses, but even in this cheap company he could do no better than seventh. The next time out he was entered in a race at a mile and seventy yards, the longest distance he had yet attempted. Here he first indicated that he might be a colt that would improve as the races for three-year-olds stretched out, for he came from behind and won with something to spare. A winter campaign in Florida netted him but one more victory and his total for the year was two wins from nine starts and earnings of less than $1500.

This was assuredly not a two-year-old to stir up Derby hopes in even the most optimistic breast. The fact that he had been entered for all the rich three-year-old classics is but another proof that owners see their horses through very rose-colored glasses. Tufano was an expansive gentleman fond of his horse and he always backed him enthusiastically when he ran. Whenever Market Wise won, champagne flowed like water around the Tufano barn.

The first of the important spring stakes, intended to prepare the three-year-olds for the Derby and the other classics, is the Wood Memorial at a mile and a sixteenth. Many a brilliant two-year-old has found this event a stumbling block, for its distance is enough to locate the weak spot in a horse that lacks stamina, particularly since it is run early in the season before the colts are thoroughly tightened for a top effort.

Although Market Wise had shown that he liked such a distance, it was in an unimportant race, and the impression was not strong enough to keep him from being an outsider at 8 to 1. The running was a different matter, for Market Wise came from off the pace set by the fading sprinters, and won by a nose in a stirring finish.

The big horse of the year, Whirlaway, did not start in the Wood. When the horses paraded to the post at Churchill Downs, to the strains of "My Old Kentucky Home," the chestnut colt with his famous one-eyed blinker and flowing tail was a strong favorite. He confirmed the public's opinion by winning by himself, eight lengths to the good in record time. Market Wise, however, ran a good race behind him, for he missed being second by only a nose.

The track was lightning fast that day, having been prepared for a record-breaking performance. It is probable that this was a decided disadvantage to Market Wise who, because of his thin-soled hoofs, always preferred a deeply harrowed racing strip. Some horses are at their best on a hard, fast track and others, especially bad-legged horses, find their legs or hoofs beginning to sting after a mile on such a surface.

The result of the Dwyer later seemed to bear this out, as well as to prove that Market Wise was a rapidly improving horse, for at the finish of the mile and a quarter he was little more than a length behind Whirlaway and going strongly. Many were now beginning to see traces of the swan in the ugly duckling's conformation.

In several races that followed, none of which was at staying distances, Market Wise failed to get up in time, although his manner of closing through the stretch made it clear that he was a router who would improve greatly at true Cup distances. When it was announced that he was being prepared for the Jockey Club Gold Cup at two miles, there was much interest among horsemen, for Whirlaway, conceded the three-year-old champion, was also being pointed for the race. Since Blenheim's long-tailed son had also shown a liking for the longer routes, the race seemed certain to be a real battle.

There is no race on the calendar of American racing that carries so much prestige for the breeder and the true horseman as the Jockey Club Gold Cup. No horse but a true stayer can win it and on its roster are most of the great names in our turf history. Although the fields are invariably small, three and four horse fields being common, there is usually at least one horse of real quality entered. So the race has always been won by good, and often great, horses.

Besides Whirlaway and Market Wise the brilliant four-year-old, Fenelon, as well as Abbe Pierre, were entered. The two older horses fashioned the pace, while the three-year-olds, both stretch runners, laid well back. Whirlaway liked to begin a sustained drive about a quarter of a mile from the finish and run over tiring horses in the stretch.

If he were to be beaten, Market Wise seemed the logical candidate for the job, for he liked to run the same kind of race and he was dead game in a stretch battle. That this was to be a real battle of giants was soon evident, for Fenelon was setting a burning pace.

He was at the mile and a half mark in 2:28 2/5, which was only 2/5 of a second off the track record for that distance! It hardly seemed possible that he could maintain such a pace for another half mile and when Whirlaway loosed his famous drive and came to him, he faltered. The long-tailed chestnut took the track to the roar of the crowd which had made him a strong favorite and another victory seemed in the bag for Whirlaway.

At this moment it was seen that another horse had moved with him and as they entered the stretch a bay horse was running neck and neck with him. All through the stretch it was a bitter fight with little to choose between the two leaders. A hundred yards from the finish Whirlaway drew ahead but before the exultant cries of his backers reached their climax, the bay came on again in a magnificent last spurt. As they went over the line it was the blinkered head of Market Wise that showed in front.

Never in the history of the famous stake had there been such a hair-raising finish and before the roar of the crowd had subsided it rose again to a shout when the time was hung out. The record of the great Exterminator, which had stood for twenty years, had been beaten by a full second!

There was honor enough for both horses, for both had given a splendid performance, but on that day, at that most testing distance, Market Wise was the better horse. He was able to give that last ounce of speed and stamina at the end of a grueling race that marks the truly great race horse.

Market Wise rounded out his three-year-old campaign on the same high note, with three additional victories in three famous stakes. His reputation might have been greater in the public mind if he had been retired at the end of that season, for he never again

was sound. In the Gallant Fox Handicap at Belmont and the Governor Bowie Handicap at Pimlico, both at the staying distance of a mile and five furlongs, he further confirmed the fact that he was **a** horse of real stamina. When he finished the season with a victory in the Pimlico Special, he concluded a season which had been even longer and more arduous than Whirlaway's.

The following year brought on the lameness that had long threatened to put Market Wise on the sidelines, but not before he had run one more race that gave notice of how good he was when at his peak. He ran a magnificent race in the rich Suburban Handicap, to defeat both Whirlaway and Equipoise's fine son, Attention, with many other good horses in the beaten field. However, he came out of the race lame, and was through for the year.

The 1943 campaign was merely a question of how long the bad leg would hold up, for it was clear that he would not last through the season. If he could be nursed along to win a few more big stakes it would greatly enhance his prestige when retired to the stud, which may have been the reason he was kept in training.

The Massachusetts Handicap at a mile and an eighth, which carried a value of $50,000, was his first important stake engagement. Although it was observed that he seemed sore going to the post, he ran a splendid race, winning by a nose in a driving finish. Moreover, he conceded weight to horses much better suited to the distance at which the race was run, and did it over a muddy track, which always militates most against the top weight of the field.

His next race, which was also his last, was as fine an exhibition of gameness as can be found in our records. As he began his drive at the head of the stretch, in the Narragansett Special, Longden, who rode him, stated that he felt Market Wise lurch in his stride and he knew something had happened. The bay horse continued his drive, however, and caught the pace-making Air Master at the wire to win by a nose.

Longden pulled up quickly and it was discovered that the tendon in the right fore-leg had given way. None but a horse of the highest courage and greatest competitive spirit could have completed the course, let alone win over a fast horse that was carrying twenty-four pounds less weight!

Obviously this is a grand horse in anyone's book and to include him under the heading of "A Touch of Greatness" may seem to be damning him with faint praise. But with the passing years the record of a horse is often stripped down to the bare facts of the number of races won and the number of defeats, without the full tale of the glory of the victories or the explanation of extenuating circumstances of the defeats. Clearly, with this game bay horse, the statement that he won nineteen races in fifty-three starts does not begin to tell the story.

The Jockey Club Gold Cup is but one of his races, but as a performance its brilliance was such that it might well outweigh a half dozen stakes won against indifferent opposition. The Narragansett Special counts only as an additional victory, but it might well be bracketed with those heroic performances of Dark Secret and Black Gold. Many of the defeats were at sprint distances, in which Market Wise appeared not with any hope of victory but merely as preparation for more important events. He was a horse that was always at his best when the chips were down, and his victories were almost invariably registered in important stake events. **U. S. 732299**

When Market Wise was retired to the stud, there were many breeders eager to have him standing at their farms. Since Tufano had no breeding establishment, it was necessary to make arrangements with someone who had the necessary facilities.

Hedgewood Farm near Lexington, Kentucky, was finally selected. With C. A. Asbury in charge, Market Wise seems certain of a successful stud career. From the standpoint of performance he should be an ideal sire, for competitive spirit—that will to race, which is so essential in colts if they are to make good—is his strongest trait. His bloodlines are also good, for while his sire, Broker's Tip, was not a top horse, his grand-sire, Black Toney, was one of our great stallions and his blood is much in demand. Market Wise's dam, On Hand, is a fine producer, for out of her five foals to date all have been winners, two of them stake winners.

From the standpoint of conformation it is also hard to fault Market Wise. His head is small and intelligent. The neck is of good length and set on the shoulders in such a way that the low carriage of the head, which trainers prefer in a stayer, is natural. His shoulder is noticeably deep and well muscled, and he is tremendously deep through the heart. He has a short back and his height at the withers is the same as his length from breast to buttock—another mark of the stayer. Every great stayer is of these proportions, often being a bit taller than his length while the sprinters are almost invariably longer than their height.

In the old English paintings and prints of horses the animals are always tremen-dously long bodied. Many are depicted as being a full foot longer through the body than their height at the withers. Since the heads were also unbelievably small in these pictures, it is probable that the artists were merely following the ideal of the day rather than the actual proportions of the horses, for the variation in our thoroughbreds today is only a matter of a few inches. The eye often sees what it wants to see and the old saying, "A long horse for a long race," very probably influenced the artist's brush.

An interesting sidelight on how a fine horseman can be impressed by what he wants to see rather than by what is before him, as far as these particular proportions are con-cerned, appears in Foxhall Keene's autobiography, "Full Tilt." Speaking of Domino, who was owned by the Keene Stables, he said that he had never seen a horse with such length of body as compared with his height. Fortunately, there are several excellent photographs of Domino, in which he stands squarely broadside to the camera, so that accurate measurements can be made. His length is exactly the same as his height!

Market Wise has the long muscles of the stayer rather than the blocky development of a sprinter, so that his conformation confirms to the greatest degree his performances. When a horse has stamina in his pedigree, in his conformation, and in his performance, chances of his transmitting it to his offspring are excellent. Besides, Market Wise had that greatest of virtues in a stayer—real speed and an ability to turn it on at the finish.

A study of the charts of all his great victories will show an unusually fast last quarter, regardless of the distance of the race or the pace at which it was run. The number of races he won by the scantest of margins, often by only a nose or a head, is in itself a measure of his courage, for when a race is that close it is often the gamer rather than the stronger horse that wins.

For those who might be overly critical of his underpinning—for he is very light boned—it might be pointed out that if ever the old saying, "A drop of blood is worth an inch of bone," is true, it is true of this bay horse. When they have that much heart they do not need much else.

Dark Secret—AND THE RED BADGE OF COURAGE

"The gallant and tragic figure of the year was Dark Secret. Driving through a sea of mud in the Jockey Club Gold Cup he fractured a leg. But with the fracture widening, and Faireno driving at him, Dark Secret lasted incredibly to win by a head. His leg was so badly shattered that he had to be destroyed."

With the passing years, the term Thoroughbred has become almost synonymous with courage and quality, although its real meaning relates only to the technicalities of a horse's breeding. Great spirit, pride and courage of the breed have become traditional through the deeds of such horses as Dark Secret, Black Gold, Troublemaker and Market Wise. They had that fierce pride of competition, the burning courage that gave way neither to despair nor disaster. Though they fought for no great causes, their stories share the pages of all those brave tales where pride is taken for granted and courage is a coin to be spent.

When Gallant Troublemaker, his chest bearing a deep gash from a splintered rail, marked with red the true course he took to the finish of the Maryland Cup, he wrote his name more indelibly into the records of that great race than did the horse that withstood his heroic drive. That tough little horse, Black Gold, was not a great one, but what he had he used. When death stared him in the face at New Orleans, long after the days of his Derby triumph, he was staggering toward the finish line on three legs.

Market Wise could not hobble the few steps to the winner's circle after his last victory, but he ran the length of the stretch on that bowed tendon. And Dark Secret surpassed even these by doing the incredible.

This well named son of Flying Ebony out of Silencia was a fine race horse in a day of great ones, for he met and defeated the great Equipoise. But his last heroic race has taken on such a legendary quality that the rest of his accomplishments are almost lost to view. Aside from that unbelievable performance he belongs with that group of unique horses which, on their best days, had true greatness.

He was a stayer, as his two wins of the Jockey Club Gold Cup at two miles indicate, yet he had vast speed and won against top-class horses at distances from a mile up to two miles. The great trainer, Joyner, said of him, "Dark Secret was the best stayer Fitzimmons ever had a hand on." When you realize that Fitzimmons trained those Cup winners, Gallant Fox, Omaha, Granville and Faireno, it is high praise indeed, particularly since it comes from a man chary of adjectives, who was a great judge of horses.

Dark Secret started on his career in a modest manner, for he was no more sensational at two than might be expected of a horse bought at auction for $5700. His new owner was the Wheatley Stable, which was trained by James Fitzimmons.

At three Dark Secret began to show real promise. He won the Kenner Stakes, the Bowie Handicap, and the Potomac Handicap, as well as several minor races. In the Potomac he beat a good field, Gallant Sir and Osculator. This was in 1932 and purse values were at a low level, where they remained throughout Dark Secret's racing career. Although he won enough important stakes to have earned a high place on the list of money-winners had he been racing today, his total was under $90,000.

The following year Dark Secret began his series of doubles in the Manhattan Handicap and the Jockey Club Gold Cup. To win one of these famous handicaps is in itself no easy task, for the prestige, as well as the purse, is a great inducement to owners of top horses. To do it twice is a real achievement.

In his first Manhattan he met American Flag's good son, Gusto, giving him ten pounds and beating him in clever fashion, with other good horses behind them. He also accounted for the Brooklyn Handicap, the Empire City Handicap, the Merchants and Citizens Handicap and the Laurel Stakes, to mention only the most important of his races.

This brings us to his first Jockey Club Gold Cup in which he was meeting the great Equipoise at even weights. The popular Chocolate Soldier had been brilliant that year but his bad hoof was beginning to trouble him. It is only fair to mention this, not in disparagement of Dark Secret's splendid victory but in justice to a very great horse. To beat Equipoise under any conditions is not an empty honor, and he was not far from his true form in the Cup.

Later in the month Dark Secret showed that his Jockey Club Gold Cup was a true race when he went out for the Washington Handicap. Here he had to meet both speed and stamina and gave weight to the field in doing it. Jamestown, one of the fastest horses of recent years, was entered and also that fine stayer, Mate, as well as several other good stakes winners.

The early pace was extremely fast, so much so that Jamestown was in distress at the mile pole, and Mate took over the lead without noticeably slackening the pace. Coming into the stretch he seemed the victor. It was here that Dark Secret, never far off the pace, began his rush and in a splendid drive ran down the leader and won by a half length in the fast time of 2:02 4/5. That sort of time was rarely hung up on that track in those days. In fact, it is not common on our faster racing strips of today.

This was a very successful season, for among the nine races to Dark Secret's credit were seven of our greatest handicaps. Had it not been for Equipoise, who cast his shadow large on the racing scene, Flying Ebony's son would have been ranked the best horse in the handicap division.

No less a judge than Jack Joyner was so impressed with him that he called him the best horse in training, bar none. His outstanding qualities were stamina backed by

intense speed and a great competitive spirit. No matter how fast the pace, Dark Secret had enough speed to be close to it and still have something left for the finish. His resoluteness and courage were of an unusually high order—there was absolutely no "quit" in the horse.

Then came 1934, which was to be Dark Secret's last year of competition, for he was getting on in years and looked valuable as a breeding prospect. A stayer with his high turn of speed did not come along every day and many breeders were willing to breed for stamina if they did not have to risk getting plodders.

He started slowly, racing himself into shape, as was his wont. Had it not been for Display's fine son, Discovery, Dark Secret might have had a double in the Brooklyn Handicap as well, for he beat the rest of the field in this event which he had won the previous year. He was also second in the King Phillip, the Delaware and the Champlain Handicaps and did not reach winning form until he came out for the famous Saratoga Cup. Here he beat his stable mate, Faireno, three lengths in convincing style.

The stage was set, the black curtain was ready, for only two races were left to the gallant horse. Fate planned the climax well so that his last two appearances were to be his most memorable triumphs. When he went to the post for the Manhattan Handicap he was attempting to bring off his first double in this mile and a half stake. Carrying top weight of 122 pounds he was in the pace all the way in an extremely fast race. He won in 2:29 1/5.

This was in 1934 when time of 2:31 and 2:32 were good at Belmont, even for stakes races. They were still shooting at Man o' War's American record, which was only three fifths of a second faster. Dark Secret had reached his peak and if he had to go it was better that he should go when he was at his very best—not after a series of defeats had dimmed the luster of his accomplishments.

September 15, 1934, found the Belmont track a sea of mud from the early autumn rains, which had been particularly heavy that year. Although this track can absorb an immense amount of water and still be fast, or nearly so, here was an unusual situation, for all Long Island was water-logged.

Only three starters paraded to the post and two of them were an entry, for Faireno and Dark Secret were both trained by James Fitzimmons. The third horse was Mrs. Dodge Sloane's Inlander, a decided outsider in the opinion of the betters. In spite of this, it would be a real contest, for Dark Secret was owned by the Wheatley Stable and Faireno by the Belair Stud. Each was anxious to win the event so rich in tradition and accomplishment.

Soon after the break, with mud splashed in all directions, it was clear that this was to be a two-horse race, for Inlander began to drop back at once. Dark Secret went to the first turn in front with Faireno lapped on him. In this manner they reached the mile and a half in 2:31, which was excellent time for such footing. There was still little to choose between them for they were running like a team. Those who remembered the Saratoga Cup a month earlier felt certain Dark Secret had the edge on his stablemate.

Now they were turning into the stretch, visibly laboring, for the test in that sea of mud had been severe. To the roaring crowd it was apparent that Dark Secret was the stronger and was beginning to draw ahead. Stride for stride they drove through the deep mud and then Dark Secret was seen to falter in his stride and Faireno came to him. Almost instantly Dark Secret recovered his stride and came on again. In a last effort he surged over the line with his head in front. A stride past the line he almost went down and after a few painful sprawling strides he came to a stop as his jockey leaped off. A crowd gathered round the horse, which stood helpless, with one leg shattered and useless, while seasoned horsemen turned away with unashamed tears. They knew that this spelled the end of one of the gamest of horses.

What happened is almost unbelievable—some say impossible. The evidence is there. Dark Secret, at the top of his stride, hit either a hole or a hard place in that muddy track and fractured his foreleg. Ignoring it he drove on and in those last desperate strides he so shattered it that there was no possibility of its ever knitting without gangrene setting in. Had he let up his effort at the time he felt the original injury, as most horses do when they go lame, the story might have been different. But if he had he would not have been Dark Secret.

To summarize the accomplishments of such a horse by listing the number of times he finished first or second and the money won would scarcely seem proper and fitting. The measuring rod for such qualities and virtues is made of finer stuff. Courage is not something that can be accurately estimated or evaluated, neither can we coldly determine if it was wisely or foolishly spent. Courage is that rare coin that returns twofold to the spendthrift but leaves the miser penniless.

Dawn Play—THE LIGHTNING STRIKES TWICE

When speaking of an outstanding filly or mare, the most enthusiastic eulogies are usually accompanied by the qualifying line, "she was the best of her sex." Rarely can the top filly of the year beat the best colt, particularly when they reach the maturity of their three-year-old season.

A big, rangy, masculine filly named Dawn Play was one of the few exceptions. After thoroughly trouncing the best of the fillies in the three-year-old stakes for that sex, she took on a good field of colts in the American Derby at Chicago and decisively whipped them at a mile and a quarter. She accomplished this in spite of ankle trouble that kept her from ever being thoroughly sound. Her trainer, the capable Max Hirsch, stated that "she never really ran but just hopped along."

Even so, misfortune was not yet through with her. With the one colt that would undoubtedly have been her master, War Admiral, on the sidelines with an injury, the rich Saratoga Stakes for three-year-olds seemed hers for the asking. But at this time one of the strangest accidents ever to befall a race horse finished Dawn Play's career.

Dawn Play came honestly and logically by her speed and stamina. She was by Clock Tower, himself a good stakes winner, who was by the imported Snob 2nd, for many years the only horse to equal Man o' War's Wither's record of 1:35 4/5 for a mile. This high turn of speed was supplemented by stamina from the dam's side, for Dawn Play's dam was Gun Play, who was by Man o' War. She, like so many successful brood mares by that great sire, was not a successful racer. In fact, Man o' War is the despair of the breeding pundits, for he so often upsets all the rules on which they build their pet theories. One of these is that you can get racers of ability only if you breed mares of quality to a good sire. Yet over and over again mares by Man o' War that were worthless on the testing ground of the race track have been fine producers at stud. That veteran among trainers, the late Andrew Jackson Joyner, finally threw up his hands and declared, "The Man o' War mares are a law unto themselves."

However, there may not be as great a contradiction here as appears, for Big Red was bred to many very moderate mares, to put it mildly, and it is not surprising that, in many instances, the produce was not outstanding as performers. The amazing thing is that so much of the great sire's quality comes through a generation later—and does this so often.

As might be expected, for she strongly favored the big rugged Fair Plays which are late to mature, Dawn Play was not very successful as a two-year-old. She won but one unimportant race in nine starts, although in the late season she gave some indication that she was beginning to find herself. In the rich Matron Stakes, with all the leading fillies of the year entered, she came with a great rush at the finish to miss catching Wand by a neck.

As this daughter of Man o' War was the feminine star of the season and there were more than a dozen highly considered fillies behind her at the finish, it was a good performance. A month later, in the Selima Stakes in Maryland, Dawn Play proved that her Matron race was no mere flash in the pan, for again she was a fast closing second in a field of fifteen.

It was apparent that she was a horse to watch in her coming season, for she was big and "growthy," as yet "unfurnished," as the horseman puts it. Such a big, angular sort needed another season before she would be herself. When she came out at three she had become a big, strapping, long-striding horse, with all the lines of a powerful stayer. Old-time horsemen likened her to the great race mare Miss Woodford, for she stood more than sixteen and a half hands and was built on the lines of an Amazon throughout.

There was nothing feminine about her appearance—in fact, at a distance she might easily be mistaken for a colt.

Dawn Play's first two starts in the spring were not successful, for the distances in the earlier spring events are naturally short, since the horses are not tightened up for the longer routes. As a result the sprinters usually show to more advantage than the stayers.

The spring activities served their purpose of getting the big filly ready for more important races, and when Dawn Play came out for the Acorn, first of the important filly stakes, she was ready to run her race. Lying behind the pace to the far turn, the big brown filly came from far back and in a long stretch drive she caught the pacemaker, Royal Raiment, to win by a neck.

The determined way that the big filly ran through the stretch impressed horsemen greatly, but the bookmakers were of the opinion that the Sir Gallahad filly, Drawbridge, which finished a half length behind Dawn Play, would be the winner in the historic Coaching Club Oaks, next important filly stake on the schedule.

In this event, at a mile and three eighths, Dawn Play had to concede eight pounds to Drawbridge and ten to Royal Raiment. The bookmakers made Drawbridge the favorite at 7 to 5, while Dawn Play was held at 4 to 1. Bookmakers, as well as most betters, are prone to judge only by performance and to ignore the potentialities indicated by breeding. Before the stayers are separated from the sprinters by performance, they were often far out of line, in their estimate.

Royal Raiment, who was strongly backed, although she was of a sprinting line, set the pace at the start. She soon reached the end of her tether and Drawbridge took over, with Dawn Play several lengths behind. At the end of a mile the big brown filly had come up to even terms with Drawbridge and soon began to drive past, going easily. She increased her lead all through the stretch. At the wire she led by five lengths.

Dawn Play showed one characteristic of a fine race horse—her improvement with each start was so great that the handicapper's weights never caught up with her. When she should have improved five pounds, according to the figures, her next race found her improving far beyond that.

Now it was apparent that Dawn Play would have little competition from the ranks of her own sex, for with each race and each increase in distance she outclassed them by a wider margin and she had the size to carry weight well. She was clearly one of those young Amazons that show up occasionally, who might well take the measure of the colts.

To test this theory she was sent to Chicago with the richly endowed American Derby as her objective. Although her size and length of stride greatly impressed Chicagoans, they had a native son, Case Ace, that was a great favorite. He was a fast offspring of the famous stallion Teddy, and now much in the limelight as the sire of the unbeaten two-year-old, Pavot.

As Case Ace had just won the Illinois Derby and was coupled with the good winner, Mars Shield, this entry was the favorite at 2 to 1, with Dawn Play the third choice at 4 to 1. Case Ace, always a bad post actor, was unusually violent and delayed the start for some time, aided and abetted by Dawn Play who evidently decided to demonstrate that the Fair Plays could compete with the best in this field also.

When the start came, Case Ace had the speed to take the track, even from his outside post position, and he set the pace to the far turn, where Dawn Play ranged up beside him. By the time they came into the stretch the colt was fading and Dawn Play came on to win by three quarters of a length without being ridden out. Behind her were Burning Star, Dellor, Case Ace, Eagle Pass, Gray Gold and Mars Shield, all of them stakes winners.

With War Admiral out of action, because of an injury he received in winning the Belmont Stakes, there appeared neither colt nor filly that had a chance of stopping this strapping race mare. The rich August events for three-year-olds at Saratoga seemed hers in advance, particularly since recent races showed that distance racing was distinctly to her liking. With this in mind she was taken to Saratoga and freshened up for that campaign. She trained well and many believed by the time of the meeting she would be ready to perform more brilliantly than ever.

On the morning of opening day a violent thunderstorm came up. Lightning struck the stable where the Hirsch horses were quartered. One horse was killed and several others were knocked unconscious, among them Dawn Play. Although she later regained consciousness she was obviously not the same and could never be trained for racing again.

Retired to the stud at the King Ranch in Texas, owned by Robert Kleberg, she was bred to Discovery, a type of inbreeding planned by Mr. Kleberg to intensify the Fair Play blood. It has been the contention of this breeder that if outstanding individuals are used, inbreeding can be successful. Since Discovery was a grandson of Man o' War and Dawn Play was a granddaughter of that great horse, this was a rather daring experiment. The foal resulting from this union was a fine-looking colt but he died before he attained racing age.

Dawn Play was subject to frequent attacks of colic after her Saratoga accident and it was one of these that caused her early death in 1944. She left only two colts, one by Equestrian, a young son of Equipoise, and another by Bold Venture, winner of the Derby and Preakness. Although mares of Dawn Play's type, which are big and masculine, are usually far more successful as racers than as brood mares, it is hoped that one of these colts from that fine but ill fated race horse will have enough of her quality to distinguish himself.

On Dawn Play's record alone she must be rated as a filly of the highest quality, but as with Bee Mac, the record is too short and incomplete for a full appraisal of her abilities. Many a horse would have gained in stature in the public's estimation had he been cut down early in his career before a weakness had been found in his makeup. If Johnstown had never raced after his Derby victory, many enthusiasts might still assert that he was another Man o' War. Had El Chico never appeared at three he might still be regarded as a great horse. So it is dangerous to try to guess what might have been. We can only say of Dawn Play that she was bred to "go on" and all evidence points to the fact that she ran true to her breeding. She improved from race to race all through her career and she never ran a race that needed explanation. Of all virtues a race horse can have, none is more important than consistency.

Every year thousands of thoroughbred foals come into the world, more than half of them fillies. Despite the most careful study of bloodlines, the most carefully planned crosses, the majority of these fillies lack the stamina that was hoped for. Only rarely does a filly come along that seems cast in the mold of the great ones of other days—of Imp, the Coal Black Lady, of the great Beldame, of Miss Woodford.

Perhaps it is too much to say that Dawn Play should be mentioned in the same breath with these heroines of the turf, but as veteran horsemen pointed out, she had that "old-fashioned" look. She also had that old-fashioned ruggedness and stamina.

This same combination of bloodlines may never again produce anything quite like her, for they say the lightning never strikes twice in the same place. It seems that this time it did—once figuratively and once literally.

Bee Mac—HER FATHER'S DAUGHTER

"When the year's at the spring" most persons think of flowers, birds and budding trees. Not so the horseman. He thinks of colts, not crocuses, of fillies, not flowers. Spring is the time when he sees the culmination of his hopes and dreams as the slim, blue-blooded youngsters first try their speed against each other in the two-year-old dashes. Each owner and trainer hopes there is a youngster in his string that will show speed to mark him as a stakes-winning prospect.

What study of bloodlines, of "nicks" and "crosses" have been made before the shy little foal, standing on his uncertain legs so close to his mother, comes into the world! No child is studied more intently or handled with more care than these young hopefuls. Potentially they are all champions, for they are all finely bred, and the most experienced eye cannot tell which will be a Count Fleet and which a failure.

When the sleek. dark filly, Bee Mac, appeared on the track one spring she created considerable stir, not only because of her good looks and smooth way of moving, but because of her very marked resemblance to her sire, War Admiral. The feats of that brilliant young son of Man o' War were still fresh in the minds of horsemen and public alike. When his handsome daughter began to show her sire's type of flashing speed she was a marked filly, even before her first start.

Her racing career was very brief, for she was seriously injured before the first season had ended. In that short time she showed herself to be one of the finest fillies in years. She not only was champion of her own sex but decisively defeated the best of the colts of her age. In doing this she accomplished more than the records show, for if War Admiral proves to be the son that will carry on Man o' War's fame, as now seems certain, his handsome daughter, Bee Mac, will be largely responsible for his success.

The story of this dark filly's racing career is only a part of the story of Bee Mac. Some of its more interesting sidelights date back to a time before she was born. It is hoped the reader will forgive the seeming digression that is necessary in order to begin at the beginning.

When a young race horse is retired to the stud the question of his success or failure as a sire depends largely on the quality of mares sent to him. Since the consensus of opinion among horsemen is that the dam contributes more than half to the success of the foal, it is apparent that a stallion can rarely make a good showing in siring winners unless fine mares are his mates.

Many persons have the idea that breeders are standing in line to book their best mares to a War Admiral or a Seabiscuit as soon as he is retired. This is often not so. An untried sire is always a gamble, for too many brilliant race horses have been failures at stud to make performance on the track a guarantee of success as a sire. A proved one, whose colts always find a ready market at the yearling sales, is a safe investment.

Had it not been for the support of one breeder in the Bluegrass, War Admiral would have received rather slight opportunities in his first season at stud, despite his excellent record on the track of twenty-two victories from twenty-five starts. There seemed to be a feeling that the Fair Play line was on the way out, particularly the Man o' War branch of that family. Most of the Kentucky breeders were looking elsewhere for newer and greener pastures.

In conformation War Admiral could not be faulted. His performance was almost on a par with his conformation, and he combined the blood of our two sturdiest American lines, Ben Brush and Fair Play. The point made against him as a sire was not against himself but against his brothers-in-blood. No son of Man o' War had proved a real success as a stallion, the best of them being only moderate, and several brilliant

WAR ADMIRAL

BEE MAC

racers being outright failures. The fact is, however, that this small dark horse was most like his powerful golden sire in the characteristics that are important to a race horse. He had much of Man o' War's flashing speed and great stamina, his love of running and his intense competitive spirit. If these qualities are transmitted by a sire to his offspring, the conformation and pedigree that go with them is of little moment.

The Fair Plays have always had their detractors. Of these Colonel Bradley, owner of the famous Idle Hour Farm, was in the front rank. Under no circumstance would he send his mares to a stallion of the Fair Play line and little of that blood was to be found at Idle Hour. His preference has always been for a smooth, medium sized horse, usually bay or brown in color. The Fair Plays are usually bright, flashy chestnuts, high headed, big boned and rangy, the exact opposite of those found in the Idle Hour paddocks.

A preference can easily become a prejudice, especially around horses. The man who keeps an open mind in spite of his likes and dislikes is most likely to profit, as the following story reveals.

With the advent of War Admiral on the racing scene, Colonel Bradley began to weaken in his prejudice, at least as far as this member of the Fair Play line was concerned. This smooth, dark, beautifully actioned colt was his type of horse. From grudging approval the colonel eventually went so far in his enthusiasm for Man o' War's agile son as to state publicly that this was as near to his ideal race horse as he had ever seen.

He tried to buy War Admiral for his stud. Failing this he booked a half dozen of his top mares to him in his first season at stud. Other prominent breeders in the Bluegrass did not follow Colonel Bradley's lead. Had it not been for the colonel's change of heart, this new Fair Play stallion would have been extremely limited in his opportunities, for there is so much Fair Play blood in the paddocks at Faraway Farm that there are not enough mares of other strains to give the stallions a full book without the support of outside breeders.

The next spring when the foals began to arrive, the colonel's enthusiasm was not lessened by the fact that the War Admiral youngsters were particularly fine-looking individuals, bearing a marked resemblance to their sire. One of the best-looking was a dark bay filly out of Baba Kenny, who had been a stake winner and a fine race mare. She was by Black Servant, he by Black Toney, foundation sire at Idle Hour. Besides her fine bloodlines and racing record, she had already had several winners among her foals, so there was every reason to hope that the smooth dark filly beside her would be a good one.

Her yearling trial fully confirmed this. She was leased to Miss Beatrice MacGuire, a niece of the late James Butler, who had been a close friend of Colonel Bradley. Under the name of Bee Mac, the filly was raced in Miss MacGuire's colors during her brief but brilliant career. On several occasions Colonel Bradley has leased one of his two-year-olds to a friend, and it might be noted as characteristic of his generosity that these youngsters were always top-notchers.

Nineteen-forty-three was what horsemen term a "filly year," for the fillies of that year were an unusually brilliant group and far outshone the colts. Bee Mac was one of the first of the Admiral's get to come to the races. That fact, coupled with her own very attractive appearance, stirred considerable interest in her among horsemen and race-goers. She not only had her sire's appearance to a very marked degree, but also his manner of performance, for she was quick as a cat and her stride was quite reminiscent of the Admiral's beautiful action.

Bee Mac's first two starts were not winning ones. Like many high-strung youngsters she had to learn what the game was about before she could steady down to real racing. Her efforts were good enough to make an impression, however, and when she paraded to the post for her third race she was made the favorite by the public. Although she was still a "maiden," as non-winners are called, she handled her field with ease and won by several lengths, going easily at the finish and not fully extended.

The handsome filly's race was so impressive that her owner decided to shoot high in her next outing. She was sent against a top field of fillies in one of our oldest stakes. This was the 52nd renewal of the Spinaway and Bee Mac was meeting a dozen smart fillies, including Boojiana, whose record was so good that she was made a top-heavy favorite. Besides being green at racing, War Admiral's handsome daughter drew an outside post position, all of which made the public decide that her chances were no better than 4 to 1.

When the start came, the dark bay filly showed the same dash as her daddy, for she outbroke her field and was close to the pace at once, despite her outside post position. With Bee Mac forcing the pace in a sizzling half mile, which finished the pacemaker utterly, she went to the front and came home in effortless fashion, two lengths to the good.

This was a really outstanding performance, for the field was a good one, the pace fast, and it was obvious that the trim, dark filly had plenty in reserve at the finish. It soon became clear that Bee Mac's fair owner was determined to find out just how good her namesake really was, for her next engagement was to be in the Hopeful, one of our richest and most important two-year-old stakes. As this event is open to both colts and fillies, it was an ambitious venture. Although the fillies often beat the colts early in the season, for they are quicker to mature, it is very rare that they can do so later on. In the thirty-nine years that the Hopeful had been run, only three fillies had accounted for the famous stake.

All three of these were exceptional mares. One of them, Regret, gained even greater fame by being the only filly ever to win the Kentucky Derby. So it can be seen that Bee Mac was receiving her acid test. Although she was meeting twelve of the best youngsters of both sexes, the impression she had made in her last race was so strong that the huge

crowd sent her to the post the favorite.

Their confidence proved well founded, for she left the barrier like a flash and took the lead by open daylight at once. Under a snug hold she ran as her sire and grandsire had before her—first at the start, first at the half, first in the stretch, first at the finish. The three lengths by which she led at the wire might well have been twice that had her rider wished. Her stride was so smooth and effortless and her whole manner of performance was so impressive that most of the crowd were left with the conviction that here was the best two-year-old of the season. It might be noted that By Jimminy, who proved to be the best three-year-old the following year, finished four lengths behind Bee Mac in the Hopeful.

A most brilliant future was predicted for the sensational filly and none could know that she was near the end of her racing career. But the next start brought the beginning of the end.

This occurred in the Matron Stakes at Belmont. A large field of fifteen high strung fillies broke in a tangle and Bee Mac was the chief sufferer. She finished fourth, beaten five lengths by Boojiana, whom she had whipped easily in the Spinaway. She came out of the race so badly cut around the legs that it was said she would be retired for the season. This would have been a wise decision, as later events proved, but since the injuries healed quickly she was kept in training and sent to Maryland for one more race.

The track was muddy and Bee Mac appeared sore as she went to the post. She got off slowly. Before a half mile was run she was finished, broken down so badly that her jockey pulled her up and dismounted. It was necessary to take her off the track in an ambulance and at first it seemed doubtful if she could be saved. The greatest of medical skill and care pulled her through so that she could be saved for breeding, but her racing days were over.

So ended a career, brilliant but so short that it is hard to estimate the true quality of this speedy daughter of War Admiral. Judging a horse solely on its accomplishments at two is difficult, for so many of the more successful ones fail to train on.

Bee Mac, however, had neither the looks nor the breeding of a quick maturing sprinter. On both sides of her pedigree, for many generations, there had been plenty of stamina, and her sire had won those distance classics the Belmont Stakes, the Saratoga Cup and the Jockey Club Gold Cup with consummate ease. The fact that she so greatly resembled him, both in appearance and in manner of performance, lends conviction to the belief that the longer routes would have benefited her rather than not.

As a brood mare at Idle Hour her value will be very great if she can pass on her own quality, or even a part of it, to her foals. That she was retired when very young should be an additional asset as a brood mare, for often the mares that have campaigned long and arduously are failures at breeding, even though they were brilliant racers. Possibly too much was taken out of them by their strenuous racing careers. Besides her individual qualities, Bee Mac has the added credentials that the Fair Plays are exceptionally successful brood mares.

When Bee Mac swept down the stretch in her smooth, effortless fashion she did more than win a race and a large purse. She, almost overnight, made War Admiral a popular sire. There was an immediate rush of breeders to book mares to him and he is now one of the most popular young sires in the country.

His fee was raised from $1000 to $1500 and his book was full long before the breeding season opened. More than that, the best of mares were being sent to him. It is probable that he will have better opportunities to make good than his illustrious sire, Man o' War, ever had, for that great horse was, to all intents and purposes, a private stallion during his stud career. Almost all the mares sent to him belonged to Mr. Riddle or to Walter Jeffords, who was married to Mr. Riddle's niece.

The desire of the owner of a great horse to retain as much as possible of that blood for his own use is understandable, but no one farm, nor two of them, have enough high-class mares to give a great horse his fullest opportunities. The reputation of the great British sires is built by such a careful selection of mates that you could not book a mare to them if she were not outstanding in pedigree and performance. It goes without saying that Man o' War got the best of the home mares, but too many of these that filled his book, to the exclusion of those from other farms, were not of the class that a great stallion deserves.

Further influence of daughter on father's career was seen in the yearling sales that followed Bee Mac's successful campaign. The few War Admiral yearlings that were offered brought very high prices and there was no doubt that the Admiral's star was now in the ascendency. Colonel Bradley was more than pleased with the results of his patronage of the young Fair Play stallion, for the other foals from the matings were also winners, and he continued sending good mares to Faraway.

From his second crop he got another filly of the highest class—one so good that she was voted the best two-year-old filly of the year. This was the fast and game chestnut, Busher, which the colonel considers one of the best fillies he ever had. She won the Matron Stakes, the Adirondack Handicap, the Selima Stakes and several minor races. Her earnings in her first year of racing were more than $60,000.

Another outstanding performer that War Admiral sent out the same year was the speedy colt, War Jeep, who won several stakes in the best company. He is so highly regarded by his owner that she paid $30,000 for a full brother to this chestnut colt at the yearling sales.

Since another of the Admiral's colts sold for $20,000 at the same sale, it is quite evident that this son of Big Red—one of his last and probably the best—will not be neglected by the breeders.

The Matchem line, to which the Fair-Plays belong, has been threatened with extinction many times, continuation of the line hanging by so slender a thread as a single aging sire. Always it has come back with renewed strength and vigor. Evidently the Matchems are not only late maturing, as is traditional with that tribe, but are also tough and not given to easy extermination, for this year one of the oldest stallions of that line, Chance Play, led the list of winning sires.

Bee Mac was a fine filly. She may well have been a truly great one. Her time on the course was too short to evaluate her properly, but her fine individuality and splendid performance brought her sire into the limelight. If War Admiral proves to be the sire that will carry on the blood of our greatest race horse, the immortal Man o' War, Bee Mac will have accomplished much. She looked like her dad and she ran as he did and that was more than enough.

Marguerite—AND MOTHERHOOD

When Gallant Fox was cutting a wide swath among the three-year-olds his picture was in every paper and the story of his accomplishments filled many columns. Almost everyone even casually interested in racing knew that he was the son of the imported French stallion, Sir Gallahad 3rd. When Fighting Fox was setting track records with his blazing speed, it was pretty generally known that he was a brother to the famous "Fox of Belair," Gallant Fox, and so also a son of the noted Sir Gallahad 3rd. But except with closer students of racing it passed unnoticed that these two horses were out of a brood mare who had every license to headlines in her own right.

Marguerite not only produced these two fine horses but, when bred to Wrack, she produced Petee-Wrack, one of the top handicap horses of recent years, and now a successful sire. All of which would indicate that she may have contributed more than a little of the quality that made her sons so outstanding.

Breeders are not slow to admit that the mare is entitled to much of the credit if a colt or filly of hers is a top-notcher. Most of them give her considerably more credit than they accord the sire. But this is reversed once these youngsters get to racing.

Around the Belmont Stud, Man o' War was known as "Mahubah's colt," but at the tracks, when his breeding was mentioned, it was always as Fair Play's son.

Pavot, the sensational two-year-old of 1944, was by the speedy Case Ace, as almost everyone knows, but the fact that he gets what stamina he has, as well as his name, from his dam, Coquelicot, is not so widely known. Since the dam is much more consistent in passing on her quality than is the sire, her importance can scarcely be overestimated.

The average stallion may sire thirty or more foals in a season and if one of them turns out to be a good stakes winner he is in the limelight. As the records show, it is usually the best brood mare of those sent to him that produces the stakes winner, for only rarely does anything outstanding come from a poor mare. When it does, there is usually high quality in her line a generation back and though it is not apparent that she inherited any of it, if judged by her racing record, it sometimes comes through in breeding.

Marguerite, a chestnut daughter of Celt out of the imported mare, Fairy Ray, has a record as a producer that is unique among brood mares. In her first start on the race track she wrenched her back so badly that she could not be raced again and she was retired to the breeding farm with only her pedigree as credentials for her success as a brood mare. Her first foal, by Wrack, was named Petee-Wrack and he raced in the colors of John R. Macomber, noted Boston horseman, who bought the colt as a yearling.

Petee-Wrack was a fine race horse who had the disadvantage of appearing on the scene at the same time as the brilliant Reigh Count. Even so, Marguerite's son won the Travers, the Suburban and the Metropolitan Handicap among other races and earned almost $100,000 before he was retired to the stud.

Marguerite had another foal by Wrack the following year, a filly named Anastasia, that never amounted to much. In fact, almost all of Marguerite's fillies have been of little value, while her colts have almost invariably been exceptional.

At about this time Mr. William Woodward, owner of Marguerite, had helped form a syndicate to purchase Sir Gallahad 3rd, son of the great Teddy, who was then standing in France. No single importation of foreign blood has so greatly affected our whole breeding structure in this country. He was a success at once and Marguerite was greatly responsible for his being in the spotlight, for when she was bred to him in his first season on these shores she foaled a bay colt with a wide band of white down his nose. He was named Gallant Fox and proved an exceptional race horse.

As a two-year-old, Gallant Fox was growthy and gave more promise than actual results. At three he was unbeatable, earning more than $300,000 in that single season. No horse before or since has amassed such earnings in a three-year-old campaign. He not only won the triple crown of the Derby, the Preakness and the Belmont but also those other mid-season classics, the Wood, the Dwyer and the Arlington Classic. He encountered but one defeat that year and it was as definitely a fluke as was Man o' War's defeat by Upset.

A muddy track coupled with a cutthroat speed duel with Whichone, finished both Gallant Fox and his rival and let the plodder, Jim Dandy, plow through the mud to a victory in the Travers. In those three great races designed to test the stamina of a horse—the Lawrence Realization, the Saratoga Cup and the Jockey Club Gold Cup, the "Fox of Belair" showed himself a true stayer. Retired to the stud at the end of this sensational season, Gallant Fox continued on the same scale, for in his first season he sired Omaha, also a triple-crown winner and a horse only slightly inferior to himself. In his second season he got the three-year-old champion Granville. A truly remarkable horse, was this son of Marguerite—one that might give her a very high ranking on himself alone.

Our heroine had now produced two excellent horses in Petee-Wrack and Gallant Fox and for a while it seemed that her story was finished. In the next five years she got but one living foal, a filly named Marigal, which never raced.

Mr. Woodward had set his heart on having a full brother to his great horse, Gallant Fox, and so bred her back to Sir Gallahad 3rd each year. Until 1935 he had no success.

Then Marguerite gave birth to a sturdy bay colt which was named Fighting Fox. The following year she had another colt which was named Foxbrough. There is a feeling among some horsemen that the brother of a great horse is doomed to failure and

it does seem that a great number of such famous relations fail to live up to the family tradition. But these three brothers were all good.

Fighting Fox won several of the important two-year-old stakes and was an early favorite for the Derby, after winning the Wood Memorial in fine style.

From this point on the record of this second Fox of the litter is quite unlike that of his older brother. In both the Derby and the Preakness he was through after six furlongs and his three-year-old season was one of disaster rather than success. Naturally, many labeled him a quitter. Those who were more kindly said he was just a sprinter, but his breeding did not indicate this.

It was as one of our fastest sprinters that he finally made his reputation, although many good horsemen assert it was a crooked leg that prevented his carrying his speed over a distance of ground. However that may be, it is a horse's manner of performance rather than the distance he can go that proclaims his gameness. The sprinter who goes to the end of his tether with greatest determination may be just as game as the horse that wins at two miles, for it is heredity or conformation rather than gameness that separates the sprinter from the stayer.

As a sprinter Fighting Fox was of the top rank and no horse finished with more courage than he. Top weight was usually assigned to him and he set track records in spite of it. Although he could never win the distance classics that his famous older brother did, it is very doubtful if even Gallant Fox could have beaten the powerful speedster at sprint distances. He capped his racing career by taking the track in the Massachusetts Handicap and leading all the way, beating a fine field at a distance that was supposed to be well beyond his range.

The third son, Foxbrough, was sent to England where he was ranked as the top two-year-old of his year, winning the Middle Park Stakes—which is the equivalent of our Futurity—from a big field which included the pick of the English two-year-olds.

His three-year-old form was far below this promise and it was not until he came back to the United States that he again returned to winning form. He was an excellent stakes winner and he missed duplicating Fighting Fox's win of the Massachusetts Handicap by the narrowest of margins, when he ran second to Man o' War's flashy son, War Relic, in a record-breaking renewal of that rich stake.

These three sons have brought great acclaim to Sir Gallahad, who is a great sire beyond any shadow of a doubt. But in this instance we can give a little extra applause to Marguerite. She proved her own worth, for she produced an outstanding horse before she was mated with the famous son of Teddy and she produced better horses when mated to him than he got from other mares.

She was denied the acclaim that comes to the heroines of the race track—Bateau, Regret, Miss Woodford and Artful. All these are widely known, but how many know who Quelle Chance, Flambino, Dustwhirl, La France, or La Troienne were? Yet without Dustwhirl there would have been no Whirlaway or Reaping Reward. Without Quelle Chance we would not have had those fine racers and great sires, Chance Play and Chance Shot. Johnstown would never have flashed that tremendous surge of speed if a mare with a dropped hip, named La France, had not existed, nor would that fleet and handsome filly, Jacola, have beaten the great Seabiscuit.

Gallant Fox's record as a successful sire rests largely on those two fine sons, Omaha and Flares—he never again produced the equal of those magnificent stayers, and they were both sons of a mare named Flambino. Were it not for La Troienne there would be no Bimelech or Black Helen and Black Toney's record as a sire would be less impressive as a result.

These were all outstanding brood mares. Their contributions to turf history are very great but none of them is entitled to a higher place than Marguerite.

Billy Barton—A GALLANT ROGUE

The development of a horse is usually along consistent lines—the game horse develops still more resoluteness, the quitter is always stopping a little farther from the finish; the rogue continuously becomes more cunning and impossible. Therefore, to depart from the beaten path, this story deals with a horse that was ruled off the tracks as a "rogue" and who became one of the greatest and gamest steeplechasers that ever raced through the field. His name was Billy Barton.

The term rogue has a wide range in its application. On the race track it means a horse that is not amenable to discipline, that will not "break" with his field and refuses to extend himself in a race. Of course he may be merely a smart horse who does not like racing and has decided to have none of it. At any rate, it is pretty safe to guess that he is an individualist.

There have been horses whose performances in this field would make Billy Barton seem a model of deportment by comparison. For example, there was the English horse Santoi, who could have been a champion except that he was so contrary he would do everything by opposites. When the field broke from the barrier he went Billy Barton one better. Instead of standing stock still he went backwards. The harder he was urged the slower he went. When you tried to turn him to the left he went to the right. Only when the brilliant American jockey, Tod Sloan, outsmarted him by accident did he run his race.

Sloan had a reputation for handling difficult horses. In the parlance of the turf "they ran for him." So it was a challenge to his skill to try to win with the rogue Santoi. However, the horse proved too much even for this skillful horseman and the field was half a furlong away before Santoi finally decided to run. When Sloan saw his fine turn of speed he thought he might at least make a showing by closing a lot of ground, so he started urging the horse on. Immediately Santoi began pulling himself up. In complete disgust Sloan tugged at the reins to bring him to a halt and instantly the contrary animal began going his best pace. The harder his rider pulled the faster he went.

Impossible as it may seem, the records show that Santoi won the Select Stakes and that Sloan was questioned by the stewards because it looked from the stands as if he were trying to "pull" the horse.

Billy Barton was not as contrary a horse as Santoi, although he was always a strong-willed fellow. Even today, in his old age, if he has a notion he doesn't want anyone in his stall it's just as well for your health to stay out of it.

He was a good performer on the track, winning several races as a two-year-old, including the Cuba Mile. At three, in 1921, he won the Cuban Derby.

He was always a bad post horse, but whether this was due to the rough handling that horses received from the starters at the old type of barrier or to a naturally unruly disposition is not entirely clear. Toward the last part of his racing career he refused to break at all and no amount of morning schooling did any good. So the stewards banned him from further racing.

Many a fine campaigner begins to turn sour or cunning after many seasons of racing, refusing to extend himself, evidently figuring that he has done enough. Occasionally one like Display or Billy Barton decides to do things his own way early in life. We may call them "rogues" and "stupid brutes" but it is well to remember that it takes a courageous horse to stand up against man, who has all the odds in his favor. It is the rebel, not the conformer, who needs the courage.

Billy Barton was of royal breeding. His sire, Huon, was by Ard Patrick, winner of the English Derby, who in turn traced back in male line to the immortal St. Simon.

His dam was a granddaughter of the fine horse Hermit, so his breeding was of the best. St. Simon was a horse with plenty of temper and many of his sons inherited it, as well as his great speed, so that the tough, willful brown horse may have come honestly by his rebellious disposition.

Shortly after he was ruled off the track, Howard Bruce, Master of the Elkridge Hunt, and a fine and understanding horseman, bought Billy, thinking to make a hunter of him. He was gelded and put to hunting and he took to jumping as a duck to water, making a great name for himself in that part of the country where brilliant hunters are plentiful. Obviously, Billy and his new owner saw eye to eye, for his manners also improved so tremendously that he was trained for timber racing the following season.

Under the handling of that skillful gentleman rider of the day, Albert Ober, Billy Barton began a racing career over the jumps that is without parallel in that field. His first start was in the Grand National Point to Point at Brooklandwood.

Stuart Rose, noted gentleman rider, saw the horse for the first time on that occasion and wrote his impressions in his book on the Maryland Cup: "I recall that as they went to the post several riders galloped out for a bit to warm up their mounts. It was at this time that I first noticed Billy, the brown gelding. Even in this perfunctory canter he displayed the most amazing ground-eating stride I had ever seen . . . I have never before or since seen a horse I liked better."

As this comes from a man who has ridden many and seen most of our great jumpers, it gives an impressive picture of the former rogue. In the face of Billy's past reputation, he was lightly considered by the hunting crowd present, which had seen many a fast flat runner come to grief over this type of jumps.

Consequently, neither the other riders nor the majority of the spectators took the brown horse too seriously even when he was over the first fence—a solid plank affair

four feet high—a length in front, nor even when he increased this lead to three lengths at the second. As one jump followed another, with Billy increasing his lead and fencing like a veteran, several riders tried to move up to him without success, for the brown horse had race horse speed. No horse was near him throughout the three-mile course and he won as he pleased.

In his next start Billy performed the sort of feat that happens only in dreams or in movie plots—and very fancy dreams and melodramatic movies at that. Many of the riders who got nothing but a view of Billy's quarters in the Point to Point had let it be known that they wouldn't permit the brown gelding to steal away to such a lead as he did in that race. Hence, it was certain there would be a lot of pace in the race, the Maryland Cup, for many horses were entered that had a high turn of speed.

Nevertheless, Billy was leading over the first fence, but was seen to swerve out to the right going to the second, which gave his backers an anxious moment. It was not Billy but the rider who was responsible, for Mr. Ober was getting into position so that he could come straight at the inside panel of the huge third fence. Even though he lost considerable ground by going wide, Billy was over the third several lengths to the good.

On around the rolling green course one horse after another tried to challenge the brown gelding's lead, but none could maintain that pace for long and one by one they fell back. Mr. Ober, meanwhile, was sitting still, letting Billy make his own pace. Then Burgoright, a fast and brilliant chaser, came with a rush to run head and head with the pacemaker. After clearing the eighteenth fence, Billy opened up a notch and moved to a length lead.

The pace was now very fast, especially so for such a course as this. The Maryland Cup fences are nothing to be trifled with, for the rails are big and strong and they rarely break. Billy, going at a terrific pace, misjudged the nineteenth fence, hit the top rail and went down. Burgoright sailed over and went into the lead, seeming to have the race won. But he was a horse at his best only when he had opposition. Coming into the twentieth fence with nothing near him he swerved and refused. Put at it again he bungled the jump, hit the fence and dropped his rider on the other side.

At this point Ferngrass, an outsider, came up. The field had many casualties that day—in fact, only three out of the twenty-two starters finished without a fall. As Ferngrass came into the twentieth fence, with only two more fences to the finish line, she looked the winner. But apparently from nowhere another horse appeared beside her, and rose to the fence with her.

As the newcomer outran Ferngrass to the next fence he was recognized as Billy Barton. Billy had been remounted, and had made up a world of ground to be again in the lead. He steadily increased his lead while going to the last fence and as he galloped over the finish line an easy winner, it was seen that the reins were all on one side of his neck. When the horse fell, Ober held onto the reins and was up instantly, vaulting into the saddle. With Billy flying along he had no chance to adjust the reins which were all on one side.

Fortunately, Ferngrass took the jump beside him at the twentieth fence or Billy might have followed Burgoright as he ran out, for his rider was little more than a passenger at this point, without the use of the reins to keep him straight.

That Billy Barton, the former rogue, took those last fences clean and true, entirely on his own, without a horse beside him, speaks volumes for that gallant jumper. To cap a story already top-heavy with improbabilities, Billy broke the course record by more than twenty-three seconds!

A brilliant campaign followed. Billy Barton was all but unbeatable in the big jumping events and he became the hero of the hunting and steeplechase followers. He won, among other races, the Meadowbrook Cup, the Pennsylvania Hunt Cup, the

New Jersey Hunt Cup and the Virginia Gold Cup. In the New Jersey Hunt Cup he was left at the post and not only overcame this handicap to win, but cut seventeen seconds from the course record. In fact, all through his racing career he did things that were unbelievable and soon became legendary. He was to hunt racing what Greyhound was to trotting and Man o' War to flat racing, a performer so outstanding that it is hard to say if we ever really got to the bottom of him.

By this time there was nothing left for him to do on this side of the world and it was decided to send him after that blue ribbon event of all steeplechases, the Grand National at Aintree, England. He hardly looked like a "National" horse to the English, who were accustomed to the big, raking seventeen handers that usually make up the Aintree fields. He was hardly larger than Battleship, known as the "American pony," before he showed the way around that tough course.

Billy soon won respect for the way he jumped the huge furze fences and his speed on the flat was also noted. The long ocean voyage and change of climate and conditions retarded him in his training so that he did not reach the peak of condition needed for that grueling course of four and a half miles with thirty big fences. Had not Americans backed him so enthusiastically in the future books, Mr. Bruce would have withdrawn him.

When the field lined up for the start it seemed clear that there was to be plenty of trouble on the course, for it was the largest field in the history of the race. The break came raggedly and Easter Hero, one of the favorites, was off in front with Billy Barton alert enough to be off well with the leaders. When they came to the dreaded drop of Bechers, with many horses already down, Easter Hero was still setting the pace and Billy was going well in sixth place. By the time the Canal Turn was reached Easter Hero was five lengths in front but here disaster awaited him.

He jumped too soon, landed on top of the thick solid furze fence, and hung suspended, thrashing wildly about. In an instant the scene was a wild melee, with horses swerving and coming down in a tangle. Billy was hemmed in and had no chance to avoid the debacle. He had to take the jump as it came.

Putting in a tremendous leap, he cleared both the fence, which is huge enough in its own right, and the struggling horse perched atop it, leaving behind an ever-growing scene of disaster.

At the eleventh fence only six of the original forty-two were still in the race and as the stands were reached the Americans were cheering wildly, for their hero was in the lead.

Becher's loomed big and menacing the second time around and took a further toll of tiring horses. Now only three were left—Great Span, Tipperary Tim and Billy Barton.

A fence or two more and Great Span's saddle slipped and threw the rider, causing the horse to swerve into Billy. Visibly tired, the American horse evaded the interference enough to keep his feet and the three horses headed for the last fence, Billy on the inside, the riderless Great Span in the middle and Tipperary Tim on the outside.

It was an anxious moment, for if Great Span refused he would knock one of the other horses out of the race.

They rose together, but Billy came into it low, dove through it and pecked on landing. For a moment it looked as if he might recover but his tremendous efforts had taken their toll. He fell heavily and Tipperary Tim was left to.stride on alone.

Billy Barton, remounted, was the only other horse to finish. Had he stayed up over that last jump there is little doubt that he would have won, for few steeplechasers could match his speed on the flat. The tremendous effort he made to avoid disaster at the Canal Turn, particularly when he was not yet at his peak of condition, would have been enough to have caused his fall at the last fence. At any rate, Billy Barton received a singular tribute, for in all the books on the Grand National, whether published here or abroad, he is the one non-winner who receives as much space and notice as the winners.

He tried for the race a second year and was well placed and going splendidly when a falling horse directly in his path brought him down and cost him his chance. It apparently was not in the cards that the great little gelding was to win this event.

Without that victory his record still is exceptional. He was good and he was game— and at worst you might say he had the strength of both his prejudices and his convictions. Horsemen that know him always speak of him affectionately as Billy. Speaking of his disposition, they say "that rascal," not "that rogue."

Bolingbroke—A STAYER OF THE OLD SCHOOL

In the early days of racing, stamina was such a prime requisite in a horse that extreme speed was looked upon with suspicion as a possible indication of lack of staying power. When such performers as the immortal Boston and his equally famous son, Lexington, were in their heyday, four-mile heats were the custom and a six-furlong sprinter would have been a drug on the market.

Gradually, as racing grew in popularity and the values of the stakes for two-year-olds mounted into the tens of thousands, the demand increased for quick, precocious youngsters that could win early. Quick-maturing two-year-olds are always of sprinting lines and so the trend toward speed and away from stamina became more pronounced.

Races were tailored to meet the changing times—and the changing breed—so much so that at many tracks the six-furlong sprint dominated the program by a ratio of four or five to one. A race of a mile and a sixteenth—a distance any top sprinter should negotiate in style—is now looked on as a route affair at these tracks.

It was into this racing world that Bolingbroke, one of our finest stayers, was born. When the sprinters are groggy and are looking for the finish line, he is just settling into his best stride. When the middle distance horses are beginning to shorten stride, he is just ready to begin his drive. He was born out of his time and only rarely has found chances to distinguish himself.

There is much misconception in the public mind on the matter of stamina. Many horses have been called stayers after they have successfully negotiated a mile and a quarter, even though they are staggering through the final furlong. If there is no real pace through the stretch, even a sprinter can stay.

A true stayer, however, does not "last" at a mile and a quarter. He improves as the distances increase. If he is not better at a mile and a half than at a mile and a quarter, he is not a stayer in the true sense of the word. And under no circumstances should the last quarter of a race over a distance of ground be run in buggy horse time. If it is, then the field is composed of middle distance horses rather than stayers.

Equipoise, the gallant, beloved Chocolate Soldier, sired Bolingbroke early in his brief stud career. Not since the days of the short-lived Domino and his equally ill-fated son, Commando, has a stallion produced such a group of racers in a few short seasons as did Equipoise. But even among such stars as Attention, Shut Out, Level Best, Swing and Sway and Equifox, Bolingbroke more than holds his own. From his dam, Wayabout, by Fair Play, he inherits additional stamina to back the gameness so characteristic of his sire. Equipoise was never completely sound during his racing career, being plagued with a bad hoof, but his son, Bolingbroke, is blessed with sound feet and legs and a strong constitution.

He is a slightly larger horse than his sire, and is molded on more powerful lines. There is in his makeup a strong suggestion of his breeding, for his head, which is fine and intelligent, is very reminiscent of Equipoise, while his body with its rugged power and strong bone shows the Fair Play blood.

Bolingbroke's two-year-old career was not auspicious. Like most stayers, he was slow to mature. While his more precocious rivals were piling up impressive earnings, he ended the season with but $240 to his credit—his share for finishing third on one occasion.

At three he had improved enough to win several races against moderate horses but that he was still less than brilliant is indicated by the fact that his present owner, Townsend Martin, bought him for $7500. This would be a fair price for a horse just above the claiming ranks.

In his second start under his new ownership, Bolingbroke began to give an inkling of class not previously suspected. Shooting high, as the odds of 23 to 1 against him indicated, he was sent out for the 39th renewal of the Manhattan Handicap. Trailing far back, as is his custom, he came so strongly in the stretch that he got up to win by a nose in the good time of 2:30 for the mile and a half. The first mile in 1:36 4/5 was exceptional for a horse that had been running in overnight races and Class C handicaps. Although he had not yet arrived, he was on his way.

A California campaign the following winter was disastrous. Although he finished third in the Santa Anita Handicap, with many good horses behind him, he broke a blood vessel in an accident and was unable to get to the races until late summer, at Saratoga. His form in several races seemed so far below his former efforts that many horsemen thought he was through with racing. As a result, he paraded to the post for the historic Saratoga Cup as the rank outsider at 12 to 1.

Trailing the field, as usual, no one noticed him until the horses came into the stretch, where he came on with such a powerful drive that the pacemakers wilted and he won going away. A handsome gold cup and $9500 was his share for his effort. Also, he had stamped himself as a real stayer, for the mile and three quarters of the Saratoga Cup had found the bottom of many a horse that lacked stamina.

The following year brought him his greatest triumph when he won the Manhattan Handicap for the second time. Although he had won this stake two years before, it was against no such field as he now faced, for he was to match strides with Whirlaway, who was then in top form.

The pace was set by King's Abbey, with The Rhymer hard after him, Whirlaway lying well back, the only horse behind Whirlaway being Bolingbroke. They reached the mile and a quarter in 2:02 3/5—excellent time even if the race had been only at that distance. Then Whirlaway began his move.

The crowd had been watching for this and rose to him, as it always did when he began that surging drive of his. Few noticed that a bay horse was moving with him. Like a whirlwind the champion came down the stretch and drove past the pacemakers, while the crowd roared its applause. Then seemingly from nowhere came a flying bay horse and in a flash he was on even terms with the long-tailed flyer, driving by to win by open daylight.

The crowd was stunned, for not only had this outsider matched the champion's famous drive, but had surpassed it. When the time was hung out the excitement mounted again, for it showed that the mile and a half had been run in the unprecedented time of 2:27 3/5, breaking the track record by a full second!

Although Bolingbroke was carrying 115 pounds to Whirlaway's 132, it was a magnificent performance for a horse which had been all out to win this same event two years before in 2:30 with only 95 pounds up. Rarely has a horse improved so much after three. Many horses reach their peak at two and are second-raters thereafter. El Chico, unbeaten at two, and Porter's Mite, Futurity winner, are examples.

Some improve immensely in their three-year-old form, as did Stagehand, Omaha and Challedon, but those that show an increased rate of improvement thereafter are very rare. Exterminator, whose superior as a Cup horse has not been seen in this country, is one that comes to mind.

Not only was Bolingbroke a Cup horse—he seemed to know it and to know what was expected of a stayer. Although he had a fine turn of speed he would never set the pace—a router was supposed to come from behind and Bolingbroke was not the horse to upset tradition.

If he were taken to the front early in the race he would pin back his ears and refuse to run. There was a proper way to run a route race and he didn't want any newfangled ideas introduced. The lead was for the speed horses, the ones he would

pass when they came into the stretch, and no one had better try to win in front on Bolingbroke!

Occasionally, as in the Manhattan Handicap of 1944, there was no pacemaker. Every jockey had been instructed to wait behind Devil Diver, a horse of great speed but of doubtful stamina. The wily Arcaro on Devil Diver set a pace that a riding stable hack could have equaled, and Permane on Bolingbroke could not have ignored his riding orders if he would. So the parade went on until the stretch, with the horses galloping leisurely. Then Arcaro turned on Devil Diver's great speed and won a quarter of a mile sprint.

If the race had been run with a fast early pace there is no doubt but that Bolingbroke's stamina and late speed would have triumphed. It wasn't run according to Hoyle, and he lost. He ran his race according to his idea of the proper way to run such a race —laying off the early pace and making his run coming into the stretch. The fact that there weren't any tiring horses in front of him changed the result, but did not change Bolingbroke.

The next time out he ran the same, and the next, and the one after that. Most of the time, if the distance was long enough to test a real stayer, he won.

Bolingbroke was soon to get his revenge, however, for both he and Devil Diver were entered in the premier distance classic of the year, the Jockey Club Gold Cup, at two miles. This time there was a pacemaker in the field, for Bounding Home went to the lead and Devil Diver elected to go with him, while Bolingbroke ran in last place.

Now the race was run in proper fashion—the speed horses in front, the stayers biding their time, and Bolingbroke could run his race. At the far turn he began his move and as the field swung into the stretch Bolingbroke went outside of tiring horses and came away from them to win by four lengths. This was a fitting climax for as fine a stayer as we have seen in many a year, for of all our distance races, the Jockey

Club Gold Cup is richest in tradition and greatest in prestige. It is doubtful if any great race in America has such a distinguished list of names on its roster, or is so free of "lucky" winners.

Equipoise's powerful bay son ran in sixty-eight races and won but fourteen of them, earning only a little more than $160,000. Many a "lucky" horse with half Bolingbroke's quality has earned as much in a couple of seasons, but such names are not to be found in the list of winners of the Saratoga Cup or the Jockey Club Gold Cup. The bay router made his record the hard way throughout. His races were the long, tough ones, with small financial rewards. He had to stay around a long time to win what he did, because there were only a few stakes each year that were suited to his talents.

Here is a partial list of Bolingbroke's accomplishments. For those familiar with racing it will be very impressive:

He won the Manhattan Handicap, at a mile and a half, three times, setting an American record for the distance. He won the Saratoga Cup twice and narrowly missed winning a third time. This race was at a mile and three quarters. He beat those two fine horses, Shut Out and Princequillo, at a mile and a quarter in the Whitney Stakes, running the distance in the remarkable time of 2:02 on a muddy track. He won the New York Handicap at two miles and a quarter, under top weight and he won the Jockey Club Gold Cup. On twenty-six other occasions he finished either second or third and in nearly every instance the race charts read, "great rush" or "strong finish." The finish usually came a furlong too soon for Bolingbroke.

To young Bobby Permane, who rode him in his races in 1944, Bolingbroke is Man o' War, Exterminator and Count Fleet rolled into one. He will talk about his hero by the hour and what he has to say is most revealing. Clearly, the horse is an individualist and needs sensitive and understanding handling.

"He's the best horse I ever rode," says Bobby, "but he had his own ideas and you had to handle him different from other horses. After the break you didn't have to take him back. He took himself back and you'd just sit still on him.

"About a half mile from home you'd feel him take hold of the bit and you'd sit against him for a quarter and then turn him loose. He didn't like the whip, and didn't need it—maybe I'd give him one crack at the head of the stretch to let him know it was time, and then I'd just let him roll.

"You'd feel him get powerful under you, just like a locomotive, and then the other horses would begin to come back to you. He didn't like to run in front and he wouldn't go through on the rail. He liked lots of room and he liked to come from 'way back.

"When you're in a race you always try to guess what the other jocks are going to do. They never had to guess about me and Bolingbroke. He'd always run his race the same—if you tried to change it you'd get beat.

"Some tracks he didn't like and he never ran his race on them. Belmont was his favorite—he'd always go best there. Especially toward the last you'd have to be mighty careful on him. He was getting a little cunning and if you did anything that annoyed him it might be all off. Just sit still and let him do it his way! He never needed any warming up. You'd feel him getting all wound up just walking. Yes, sir, he was a horse!"

At the end of the 1944 season Bolingbroke was retired from racing at the age of seven. His admirers were greatly heartened when it was learned that he would stand as a stallion at Coldstream Stud in Kentucky.

The announcement shortly after, that his book for 1945 was full, is most encouraging, for here is a sire that is eminently fitted to bring stamina to pedigrees that are top-heavy with sprinting blood. He combines the blood of two of our greatest sires—Equipoise and Fair Play—and he was himself a magnificent performer. His story may be just beginning.

Wise Counsellor

FROM THE WRONG SIDE OF THE TRACKS

If the average horseman or breeder were asked what qualifications he would look for in a sire, he would undoubtedly say the ability to get colts and fillies that are winners, for fine breeding without good performance to back it up is of little value. He might add that he would prefer good names in his pedigree. But the prime requisite would be good performance on the race course and an ability to sire winners at stud.

Yet one of our stallions who more than fulfilled these requirements was not a popular sire and never had a real opportunity to prove his true worth.

He was beaten but once in five starts, as a two-year-old when he finished second. He was good enough to beat the brilliant French horse, Epinard, as well as Black Gold, Mad Play, and that speed hound, Chilhowee

Despite the fact that he never had top class mares sent to him, for five years he led all sires in number of winners and number of races won.

Fashionable breeders avoided Wise Counsellor as if his blood were poison and yet he stemmed in male line from one of the greatest racers that ever stepped on a course. Even in death he was the poor boy from the wrong side of the tracks, for his death was due to an accident that probably never would have happened to a fashionable imported stallion. This last outstanding member of the great Glencoe line made good against vast odds, but it did not raise him to the heights. Like the Red Queen, he had to run his fastest merely to stay where he was.

The story of Wise Counsellor is a story of breeding, for although he was a fine race horse, it is as a sire that he was phenomenal. At one time, in the latter part of the 1800's, the Glencoe line was one of the most powerful and fashionable in America.

Then it began to die out and only by chance was it revived to write a few more brilliant chapters in turf history.

Twice the line was on the point of complete extinction and twice it was revived— once by the immortal Hindoo and again by his great-great-grandson, Wise Counsellor. Whether another son will come out of obscurity and again give life to that once great line is a matter for the future.

The Glencoe line had fallen so far from favor that one of the last stallions of that line, Virgil, was used mostly as a buggy horse around the Preakness Stud. The black stallion was occasionally bred to a few nondescript mares. After the breeding season he was given away, but when several of his colts began to show far more speed than those of the top stallions on the farm, he was brought back and given better mares.

From this crop, in 1878, came Hindoo. All horsemen who saw Hindoo race through his severe and amazing career consider him one of the greatest horses ever foaled in this country and more than one of them consider him the greatest of all, not excluding Man o' War. He ran thirty-five races and won thirty of them, usually under top weight, and was never unplaced in his entire career.

He was that ideal of all horsemen—a horse of stamina with the speed of a sprinter. He beat the sprinters at six furlongs and the stayers at two miles and a quarter. Had he been raced by any other stable than that of the Dwyer brothers, his record would have been even more impressive, for those heavy plungers, nicknamed "The Butcher Boys," thought nothing of the welfare of a horse if a big bet could be won. Often Hindoo had only a day or two of rest between hard races.

As a stallion Hindoo was a great success, getting among other good horses the brilliant Hanover, a horse only slightly inferior to himself. At stud Hanover got good horses, but the Glencoe line began to go into eclipse when his best sons died early and the few remaining ones failed to "breed on."

Hanover's death was indirectly due to a practice which is now severely criticized by horsemen. In order to overcome a recurrent lameness in a forefoot, Hanover was "nerved." In this operation the nerve that runs to the foot is severed so that a horse feels no pain in it. The result of this is often a severe fracture of the leg, for the horse receives no warning of any weakness there.

Hanover had been suffering from stomach trouble and while he was recovering it had been necessary to restrict his diet. Always a voracious feeder, as are most great horses, he showed his impatience with his limited diet by stamping in his stall. Since there was no pain to warn him, he stamped so violently that he broke a bone in his foot. Every attempt was made to save him, but gangrene set in and it was necessary to destroy him.

Again fate seemed to have stacked the cards against the once famous line, for with the passing of Hanover the story of the Glencoe strain seemed finished.

Once a great line begins to fade its descent into obscurity is accelerated by the breeders, for they are very quick to veer away from it and follow the newest success. It would seem that an effort should be made to revive bloodlines that had proved great in the past, for there might still be an ember that could be nursed to a glowing flame. But the attempt is rarely made. It is more often a case of "The King is dead, long live the King."

Possibly because there is so much that happens in breeding that cannot be explained by "nicks," "crosses," bloodlines, or racing records, most breeders are eager to try out the newest successful stallion, always hoping to find the happy combination that produces champions.

Of the sons left by Hanover, many were more promising than Blackstock, yet it was through him that the line again emerged into the racing spotlight. He in turn sired a colt named Mentor, who ended his career as a remount stallion in Wyoming, siring hunters and cow horses. From this more than obscure sire and out of a mare of so little note that she sold for $100 while carrying the foal that was Wise Counsellor, came one of our most brilliant milers, and a sire so prepotent that he passed on his speed, regardless of the mares to which he was mated. Rarely, if ever, has a stallion accomplished so much with such limited opportunities.

In 1920, at a horse auction in Lexington, Kentucky, a group of nondescript horses in poor condition and of obscure breeding were put up for sale. They came from a small breeder in Missouri and the prices they brought seemed to indicate that they were weedy farm stock rather than Thoroughbreds.

Among them was a fifteen-year-old mare named Rustle, in foal to an obscure stallion named Mentor. In the Bluegrass, where pedigrees fairly bristle with great names, such a horse would be hard to give away. Mr. Charles Berryman, who owned Ballot, a very popular stallion of the day, told his friend, Thomas C. Bradley, that he would give him a service to Ballot if he cared to buy the old mare. With this encouragement Mr. Bradley bid $100 and got the mare.

In the spring Rustle dropped a chestnut foal, well marked with white, that was named Wise Counsellor. This was not only an appropriate name for a son of Mentor, but proved doubly appropriate later for his owner states that the chestnut colt was the most intelligent and best mannered horse he had ever known. His post behavior was almost as faultless as that of Exterminator and Mr. Bradley says that he used such intelligence in his eating and resting after workouts that he almost conditioned himself. This intelligence and good behavior were transmitted to his offspring almost as unfailingly as the speed for which they were noted.

In yearling trials the chestnut colt showed unusual speed and the next spring he created a mild sensation at Churchill Downs by working a half mile a fifth of a second faster than the track record. Mr. Bradley now knew he had picked up a bargain but

just how great a bargain was yet to be revealed.

In his first start, although green at the game, Wise Counsellor was a good second. From then on he was unbeaten that season. In four races he conquered such horses as Black Gold, Mad Play and Chilhowee, all of whom became stars. The last two races were at a mile, which is a very fair distance for a two-year-old. Many breeders stigmatized Wise Counsellor as a mere sprinter with a short tether, but some of our popular sires were never top milers, even at maturity, being better suited to six and seven furlongs.

By this time Wise Counsellor was such a sensation that large offers were being made for him. Mr. Bradley, who raced on a modest scale, felt that the horse had become too important a figure for his kind of racing. When $66,000 was offered for Wise Counsellor, Mr. Bradley accepted.

As a three-year-old Wise Counsellor met the best horses in training and had his share of victories.

In conformation he was definitely a sprinter, being long bodied compared to his height. He carried his speed in top style up to a mile, and he could undoubtedly have been stretched a furlong beyond that if especially prepared for it. He twice defeated the French invader, Epinard, once in the First International Special at six furlongs and again in the Laurel Stakes at a mile. In the Laurel Stakes he also beat such top horses as Big Blaze, My Play and Sun Flag. In all, he started twenty-two times, won ten races and was out of the money but five times. He was a good weight carrier and was a consistent performer. He was, in short, the type of horse that might be expected to be popular as a stallion.

If Wise Counsellor had stood in England, where stamina is paramount in their breeding scheme, it would be understandable that he might not be popular. But in the United States, where half of our sires are sprinters, it is harder to fathom. Particularly does this seem strange when he began sending out a larger proportion of winners from commonplace mares than many big-name sires were getting from stakes-winning brood mares. It is true, of course, that his pedigree was most unfashionable, but since he was so much superior to his immediate ancestors, it could well be assumed that he might be a truer descendant of Hanover than either his sire or his grandsire.

Among horses, as among people, quality is apparently not transmitted for a generation or two. Then it occasionally appears strongly again. It would even seem that blood which could survive under such unfavorable conditions should be held at a premium, for many strains have failed to survive despite the greatest of opportunities.

Perhaps the great vogue for imported stallions of impressive pedigrees was as much responsible for the breeders' neglect of Wise Counsellor as any other factor. All our native lines were left to play second fiddle, particularly those whose pedigrees were a bit homespun. However, on that testing ground, the race track, our native strains are coming forward so strongly again that if Wise Counsellor had lived a few more years his real opportunity might have come.

An experienced trainer unburdened himself on the subject recently, when he said, "If the pedigree students had to race the foals which result from their fads and fancies, I believe they would concentrate more on mating horses that have shown the instinct to race and less on achieving a pretty pedigree. If a stallion or mare is not himself or herself intuitively a race horse, the chances of getting a runner as a foal are remote, no matter how many rich relatives they may have."

Right from the start Wise Counsellor began sending out winners. In his first season he had only two foals and both won. The next year there were seven, of which five won. In 1929, he got his first stakes winner and the following year there were four stakes winners, with nearly all the rest winners of races.

The next year, 1931, brought a perfect score with twelve winners out of twelve foals, one of them the good stakes-winning filly, Wise Daughter. From then on he struck an average of seventy-five per cent winners among his foals—a mark he maintained to the end of his career.

Among these were the stakes winners Uncovered, Wise Anne, Sandy Bill, Marie Jean, Good Advice, Wise Daughter, and that handsome speedster which is now siring winners, Deliberator. Also, he got the stakes winners Wise Prince, Wise Bessa, Supreme Court, Sound Advice, Wise Duke, Jay Jay, Appealing, Family Friend, Wise Mentor, Dale K, Wise Bee, Teacher, Nannykins, Wise Moss—who soundly whipped the New England sprinting sensation, Sweet Willow, in a match race—Wise Bob, Wise Niece and Trustee. All were favorably known to race goers as fast and very consistent horses.

Two of his offspring, Ogham and Surrogate, were two-year-old stakes winners in 1943.

Wise Counsellor's twenty-seven stakes winners out of 264 foals was an amazing percentage when we consider that most of his mares would not be found acceptable in the books of the fashionable sires. To the end of 1943 his get had won more than $1,600,000 and the full score is not yet in, for many a Wise Counsellor colt and filly is still entering the winner's circle.

It has been said that "the Wise Counsellors are looking too hard for the finish pole after six furlongs," but the same could be said with even more truth of the Ariels and the Bull Dogs. Most sprinting sires tend to produce horses of even shorter tether than themselves. Even when mated with mares of staying lines, little additional range seems to be added. If a sire is of sprinting blood for many generations, the chances of his producing a true stayer are very remote. If, however, his sprinting tendencies are due to conformation and not heredity there is a very fair chance of getting horses of greater stamina; if bred to mares of stamina, for conformation is not always transmitted.

A little sidelight on this point, as it relates to Wise Counsellor, might be of interest.

As with all stories of breeding it is necessary to digress and go back a bit to get the salient facts.

Crow's Feet was a Man o' War mare that was unable to win on the track. One of her daughters produced a filly of highest class and amazing speed when bred to Wise Counsellor. This filly, named Hauca, was sweeping the boards among two-year-olds of her sex, completely distancing her fields. She had to be destroyed after a fall at Saratoga that broke a leg. Her class was so outstanding that in an attempt to follow the same "nick," Crow's Feet was bred to Wise Counsellor.

The well named chestnut colt, No Wrinkles, that resulted from this mating, showed clearly what Wise Counsellor could do when crossed with stamina, for the colt won two races at a mile and an eighth in four days, one of them a handicap. Another mating of Crow's Feet and Wise Counsellor produced Go Chicago, a consistent winner in purse events and able to get distances well above a mile. Sprinting blood pure and simple does not respond in this manner to a cross with stamina.

Several of Wise Counsellor's sons are at stud. Among them Deliberator and Good Advice from very limited opportunities seem to have made a good start as stallions. Three Dots, a son of Good Advice, showed some of his grandsire's speed by three times beating Occupation, winner of the Futurity over Count Fleet and rated by most horsemen as Bull Dog's best son of recent years. Deliberator has also sent out some nice colts. Since he is a horse of great beauty, he may receive patronage from those who faulted his sire's conformation.

A cross of Wise Counsellor speed with stamina through a top-class Fair Play mare might have produced something very good, judging from the evidence given above. Perhaps one of Wise Counsellor's sons will be given the opportunity his sire never had.

Briefly, here is the record of the chestnut stallion that "didn't belong": He has ten times been among the twenty leading sires, estimated by the earnings of their offspring. Five times he has led the list in number of winners and races won. Twice he has led the list as sire of two-year-old winners. Seventy-five per cent of all his foals have been winners and ten per cent have been stakes winners. All this has been accomplished when he was bred to mares whose inferiority to those bred to popular stallions would be hard to underestimate.

When all is said and done, you can believe that here is a success story that is different. The poor boy met great obstacles, surmounted them and was still regarded as a failure. Even on his home farm he was no hero. His death was due to a fractured leg, caused by a kick he received from a carelessly hobbled mare in the breeding shed.

Nevertheless, his record still stands and many a glowing description of the accomplishment of a fashionable, popular sire is based on far less. He may not have been truly great but assuredly there was greatness in him.